BIG-NOTE PIANO

Worship Favorites

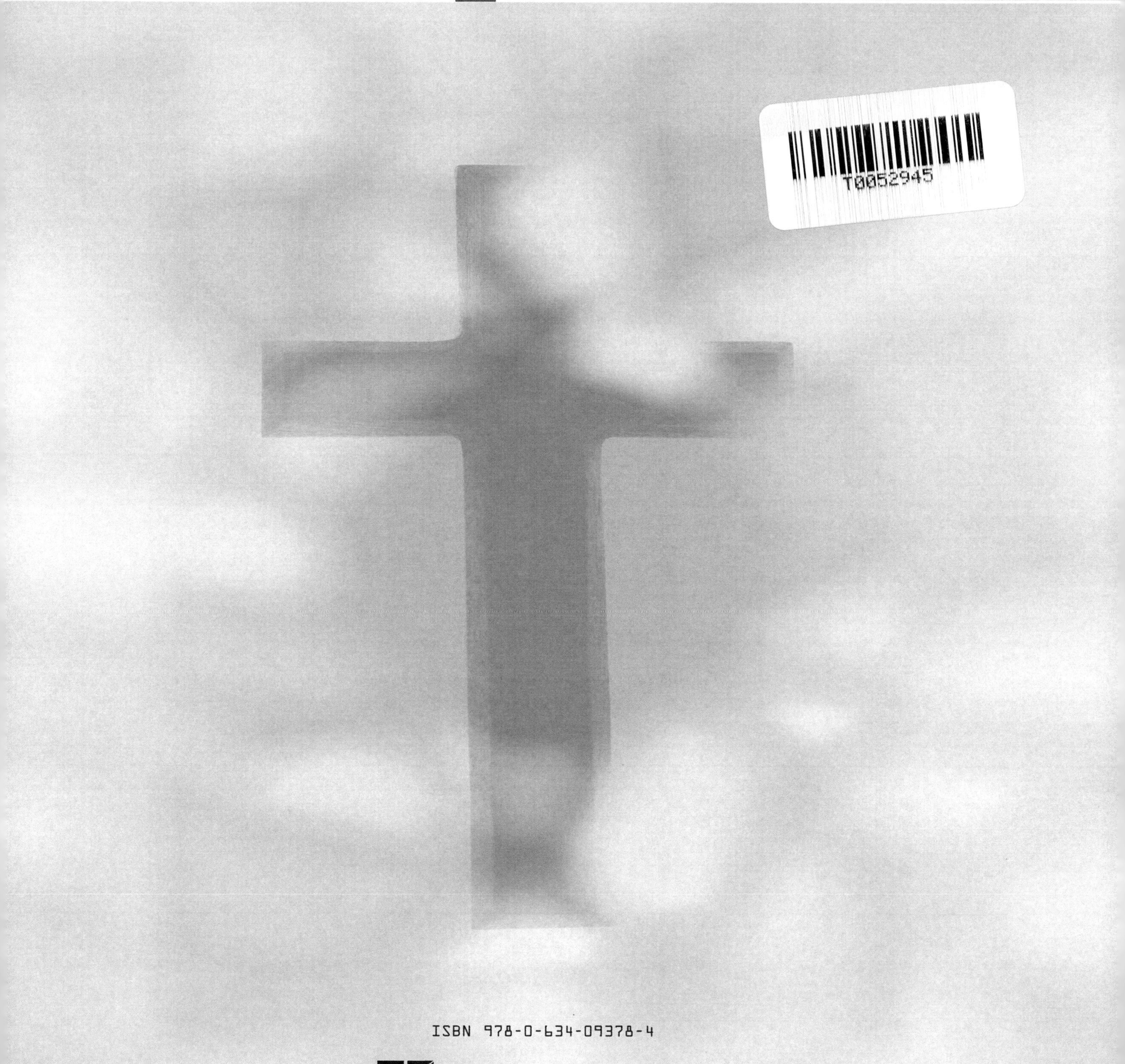

T0052945

ISBN 978-0-634-09378-4

7777 W. Bluemound Rd. P.O. Box 13819 Milwaukee, WI 53213

Visit Hal Leonard Online at
www.halleonard.com

ABOVE ALL

Words and Music by PAUL BALOCHE
and LENNY LeBLANC

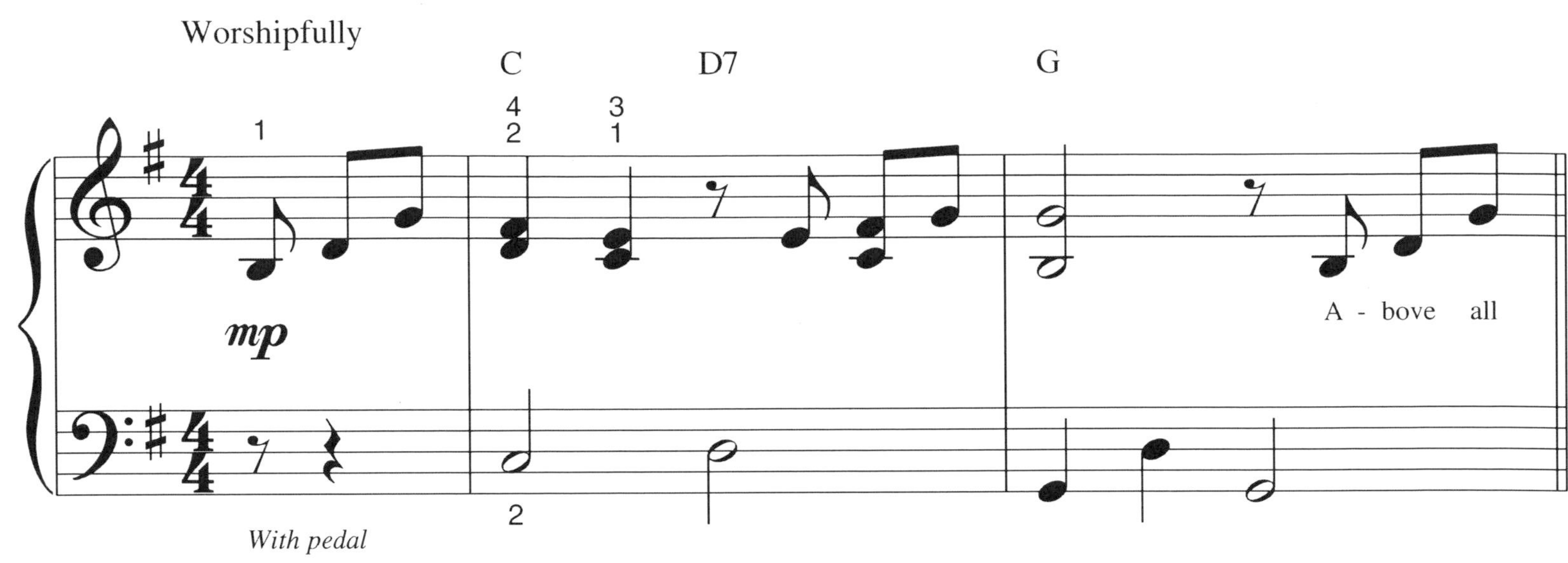

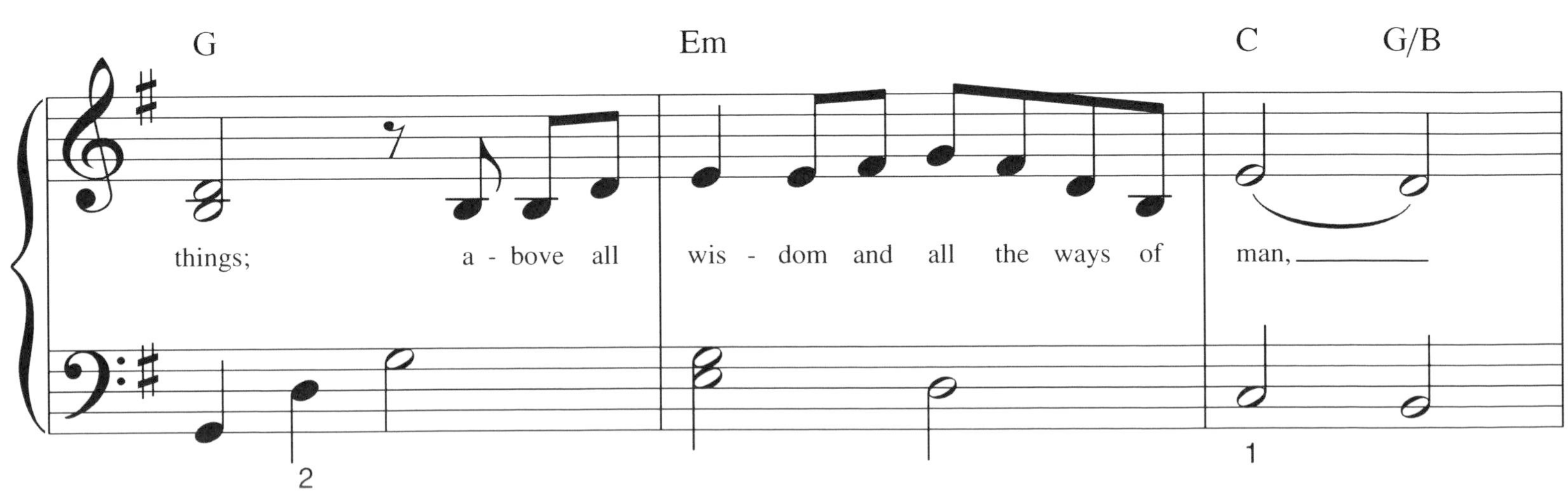

Am C/G D/F♯ G C D7
1 2 1 1
You were here be - fore the world be - gan. A - bove all king - doms, a - bove all
2
G C D7 G
thrones, a - bove all won - ders the world has ev - er known; a - bove all
Em C G/B Am C/G
1 2
wealth and treas - ures of the earth, there's no way to meas - ure what You're
1
Bsus B G Am7 D/F♯ G
3
worth. Cru - ci - fied, laid be - hind a stone, You
4

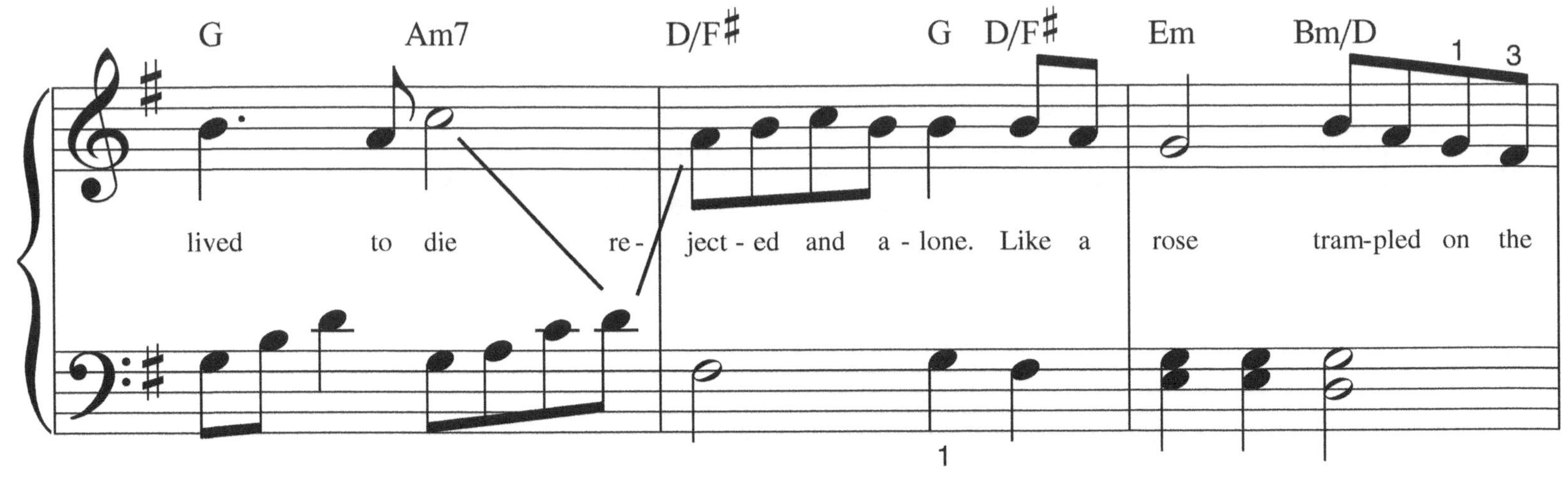
G
Am7
D/F♯
G
D/F♯
Em
Bm/D
lived to die re - ject - ed and a - lone. Like a rose tram-pled on the

To Coda
C
G/B
Am7
G/B
C
D
ground, You took the fall and thought of me a - bove

1.
G
Em
G/D
C
D7
all.

2.
D.S. al Coda
G
C/E
D/F♯
A - bove all
all.
CODA
G
Em
Bm/D
all.
Like a
rose
tram - pled on the
C
G/B
Am7
G/B
C
D
ground, You took the
fall
and thought of
me
a - bove
G
C
Dsus
D
G
all.
rit.

BETTER IS ONE DAY

Words and Music by
MATT REDMAN

F5
B♭sus2
here my heart is sat - is - fied with - in Your pres -
thing I ask and I would seek: to see Your beau -

Csus
F5
5 3
- ence. I sing be - neath the shad - ow of Your
- ty, to find You in the place Your glo - ry

Csus
C
B♭sus2
1 2 4
wings.
dwells.
Bet-ter is one day in Your courts, bet-ter is

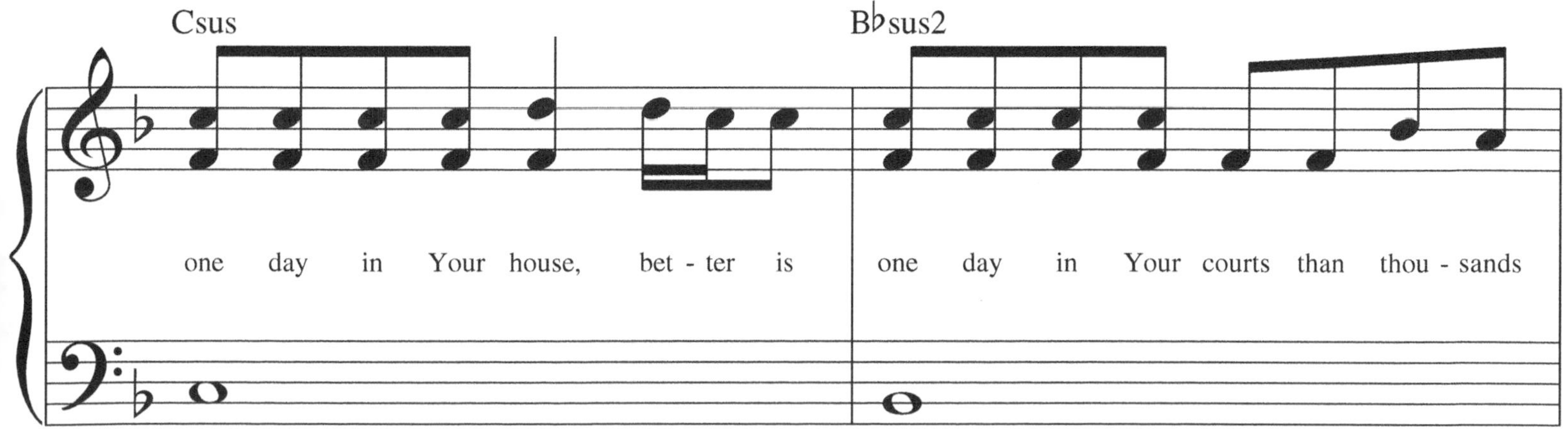
Csus
B♭sus2
one day in Your house, bet - ter is one day in Your courts than thou - sands

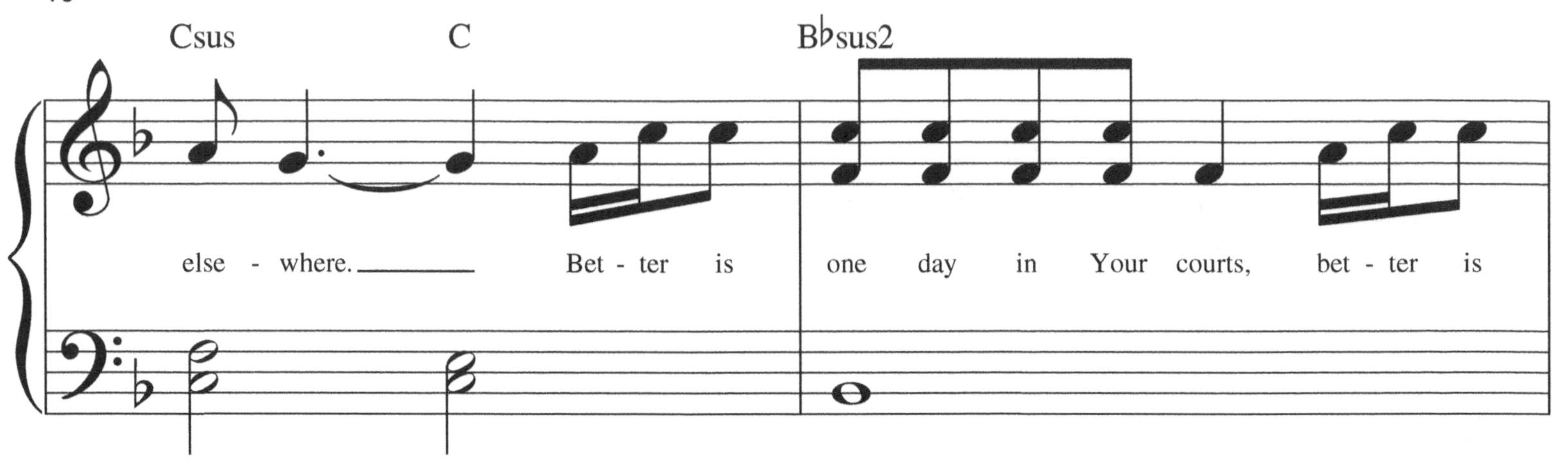
Csus
C
B♭sus2
else - where.
Bet - ter is
one day in Your courts,
bet - ter is

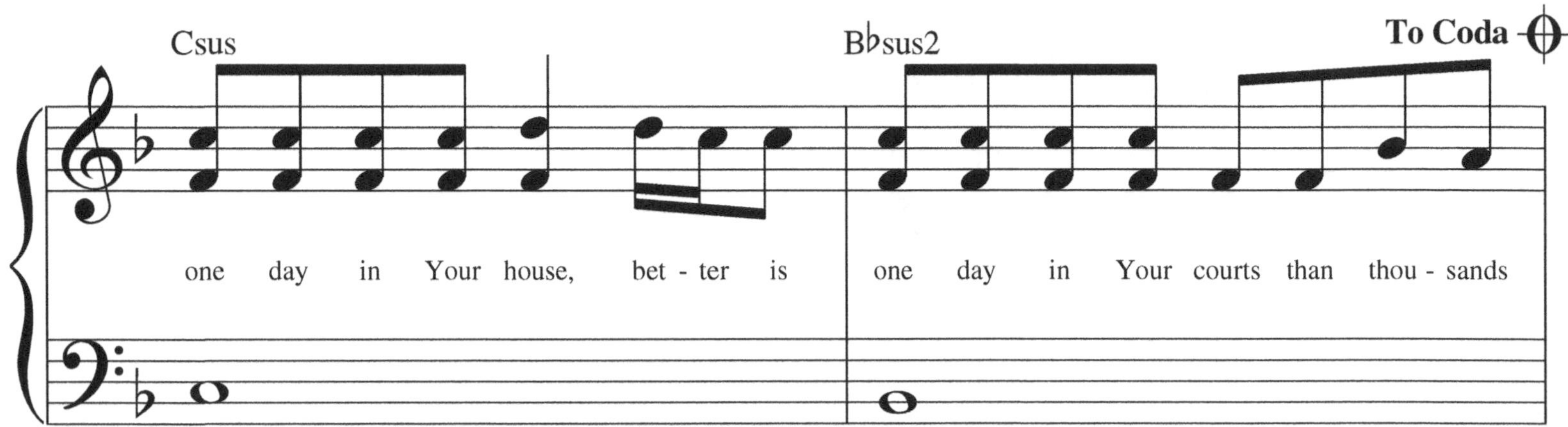
Csus
B♭sus2
To Coda
one day in Your house,
bet - ter is
one day in Your courts than thou - sands

1.
Csus
C
F5
4
else - where,
than thou - sands
else - where.
One

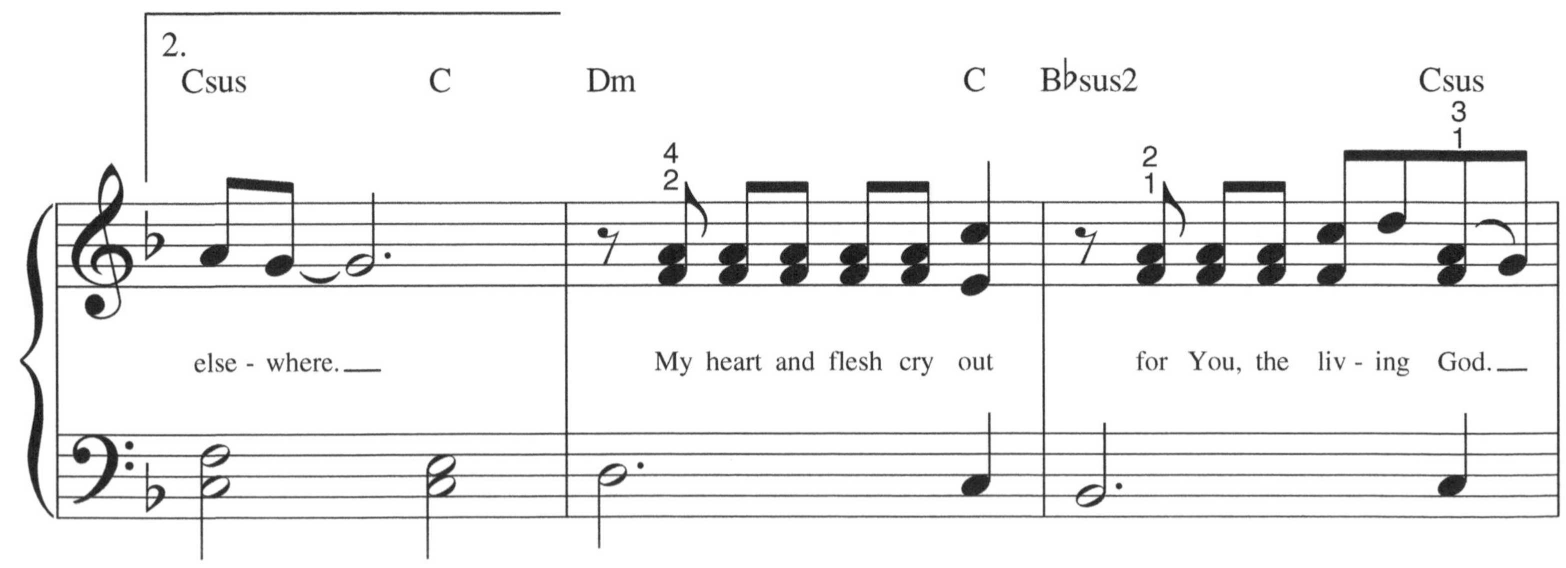
2.
Csus
C
Dm
C
B♭sus2
Csus
4
2
2
1
3
1
else - where.
My heart and flesh cry out
for You, the liv - ing God.

Dm
Csus
Bbsus2
Csus
Dm
C
4
1
Your Spir - it's wa - ter to my soul.
I've tast - ed and I've seen,

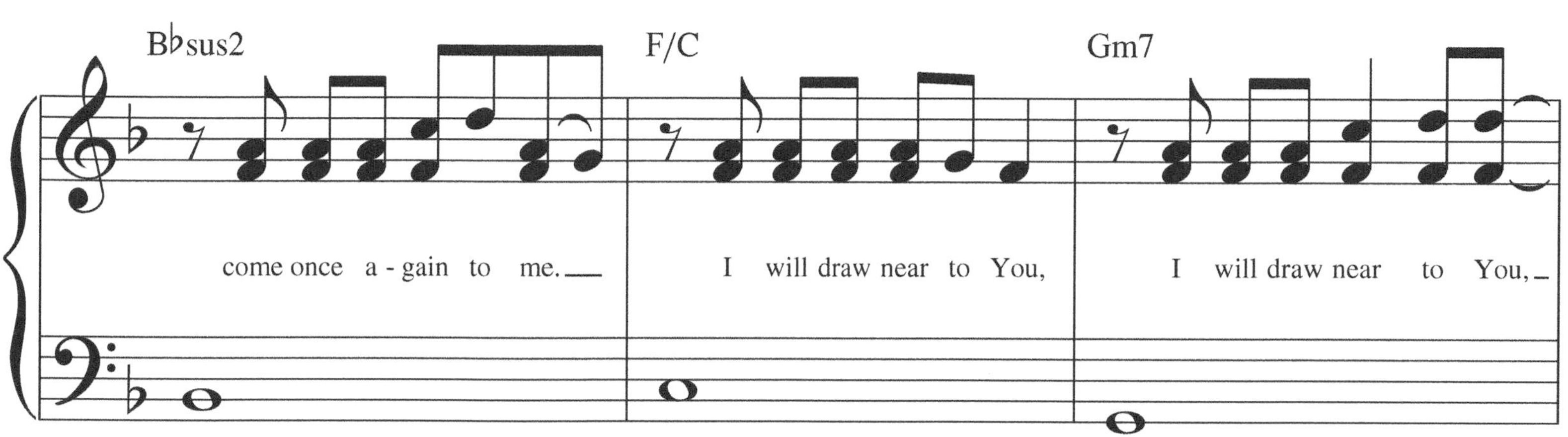
Bbsus2
F/C
Gm7
come once a - gain to me.
I will draw near to You,
I will draw near to You,

C7sus
Bbsus2
to You.

Csus
Bbsus2
Csus
2 4
Bet - ter is

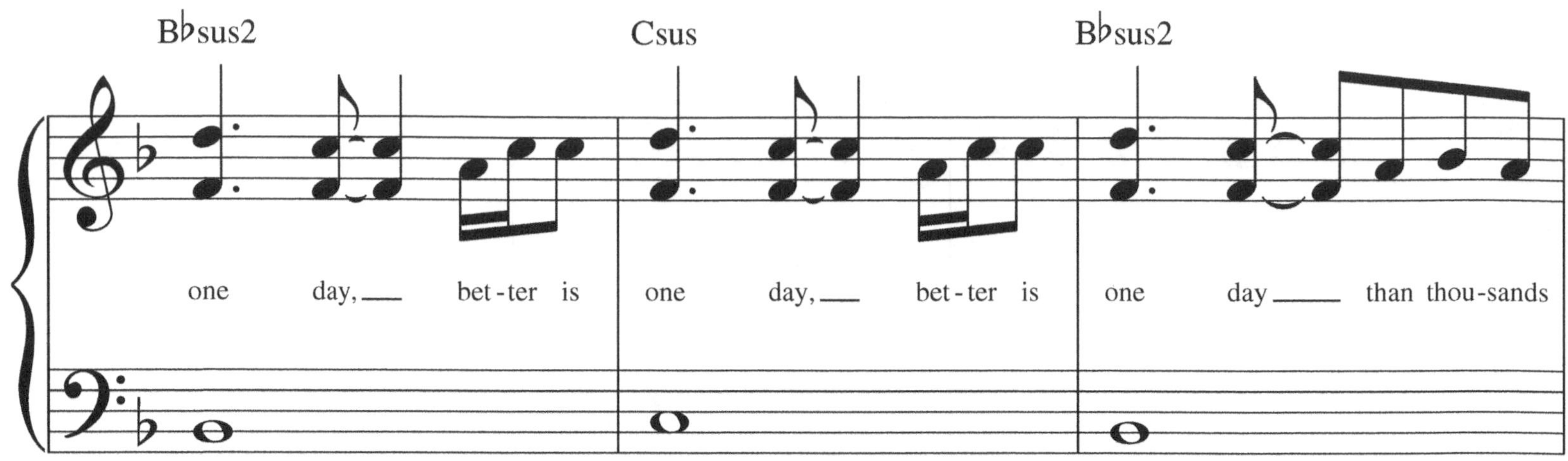
B♭sus2
Csus
B♭sus2
one day, bet-ter is one day, bet-ter is one day than thou-sands

Csus
C
B♭sus2
else - where. Bet - ter is one day, bet - ter is

Csus
B♭sus2
one day, bet - ter is one day than thou - sands

Csus
C
D.S. al Coda
else - where. Bet-ter is

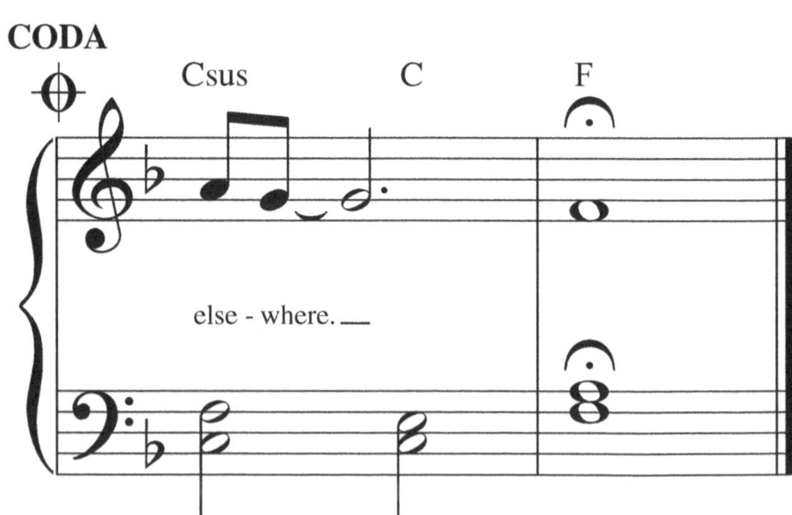
CODA
Csus
C
F
else - where.

DRAW ME CLOSE

Words and Music by
KELLY CARPENTER

Worshipfully

C F/C G/C

1

mf

With pedal

F/C C F/C

Draw me close to You,

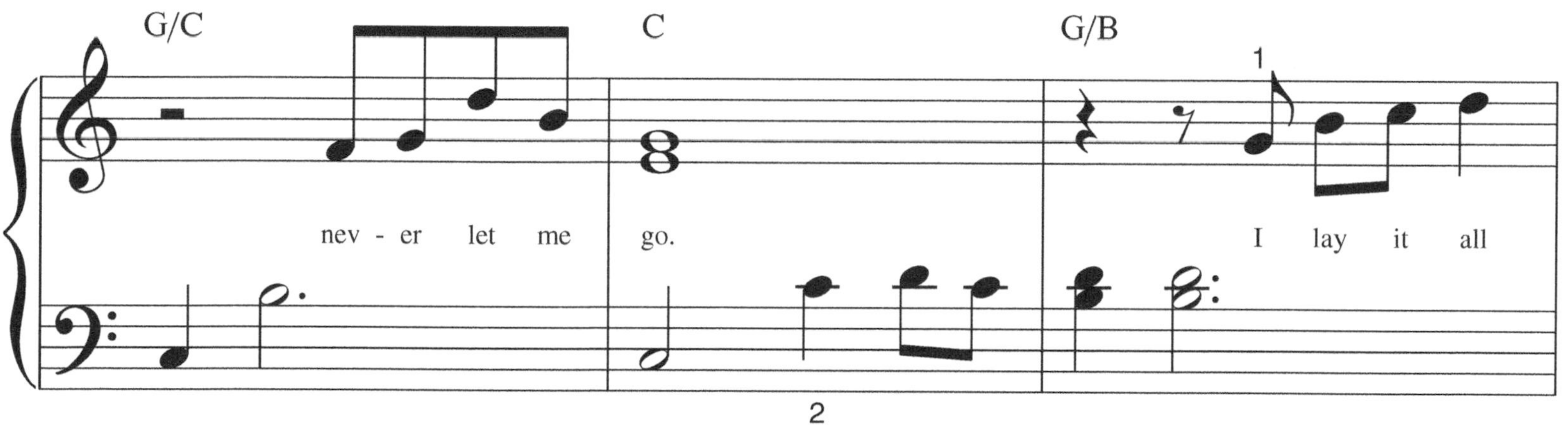

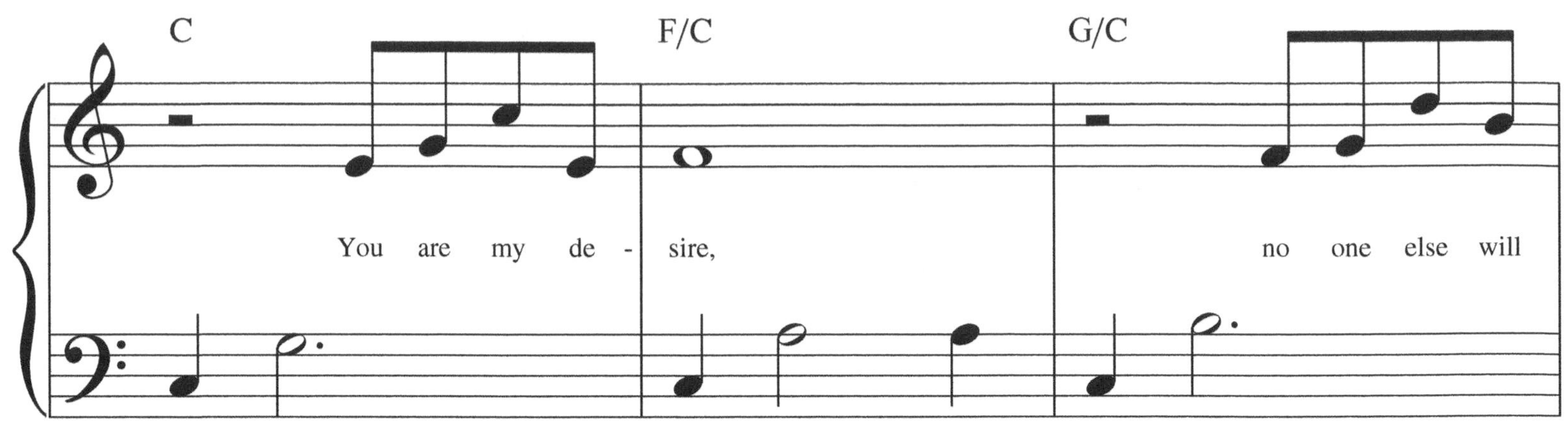
C
F/C
G/C
You are my de - sire, no one else will

C
G/B
F/A
1
do. 'Cause noth - ing else could take Your place

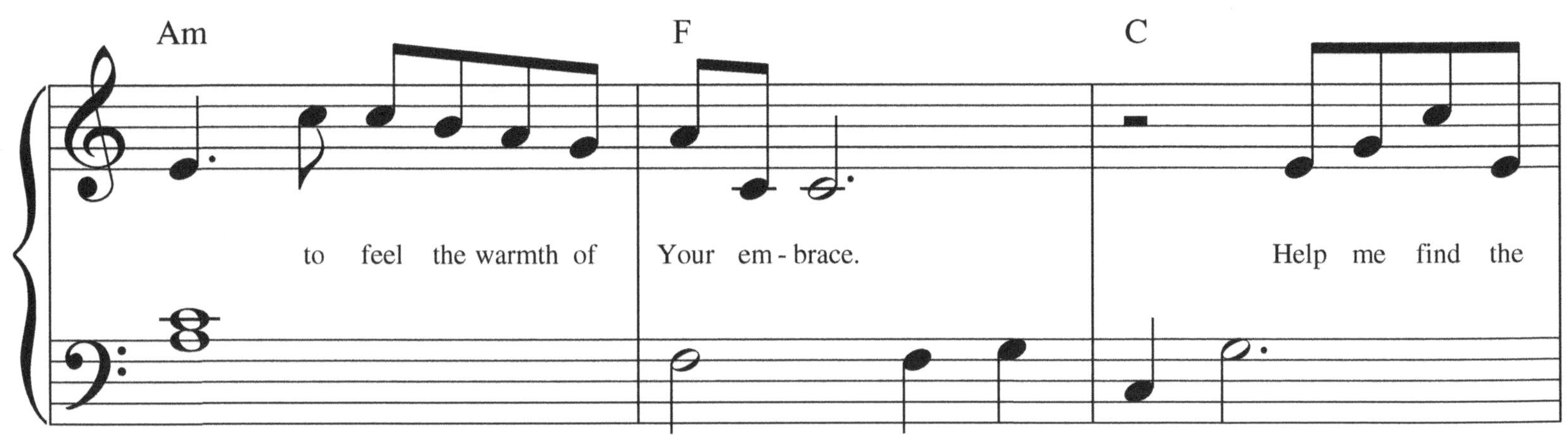
Am
F
C
to feel the warmth of Your em - brace. Help me find the

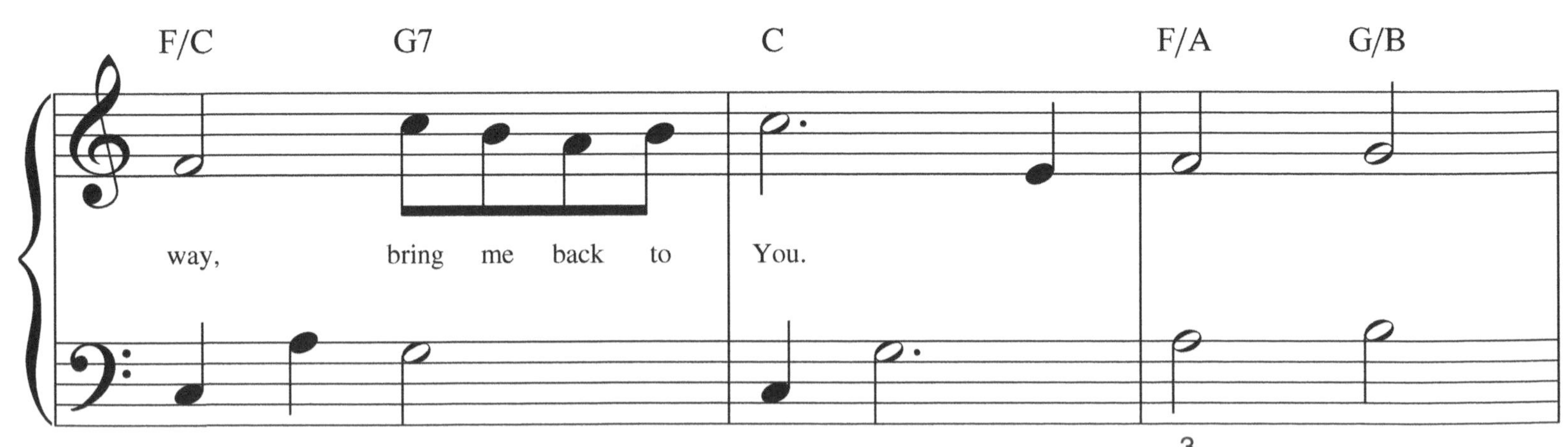
F/C
G7
C
F/A
G/B
way, bring me back to You.

3

C G F C G
You're all I want, You're all I've
F G Am G F C/E
ev - er need - ed. You're all I want.
1.
2.
D.S. al Coda
Dm7 G7 To Coda C C F/G G
Help me know You are near. near.
CODA
Am Dm7 G7 C
near. Help me know You are near.
rit.

BREATHE

Words and Music by
MARIE BARNETT

D
G
D/F♯
Em
D
And
I,
I'm lost with -
To Coda
D.C. al Coda
(with repeat)
CODA
C
Em
D
out You.
D
I'm lost with -
C
Em
D
C
Em
out You,
I'm lost with -
out You.
D
C
3
Em
D

COME, NOW IS THE TIME TO WORSHIP

Words and Music by
BRIAN DOERKSEN

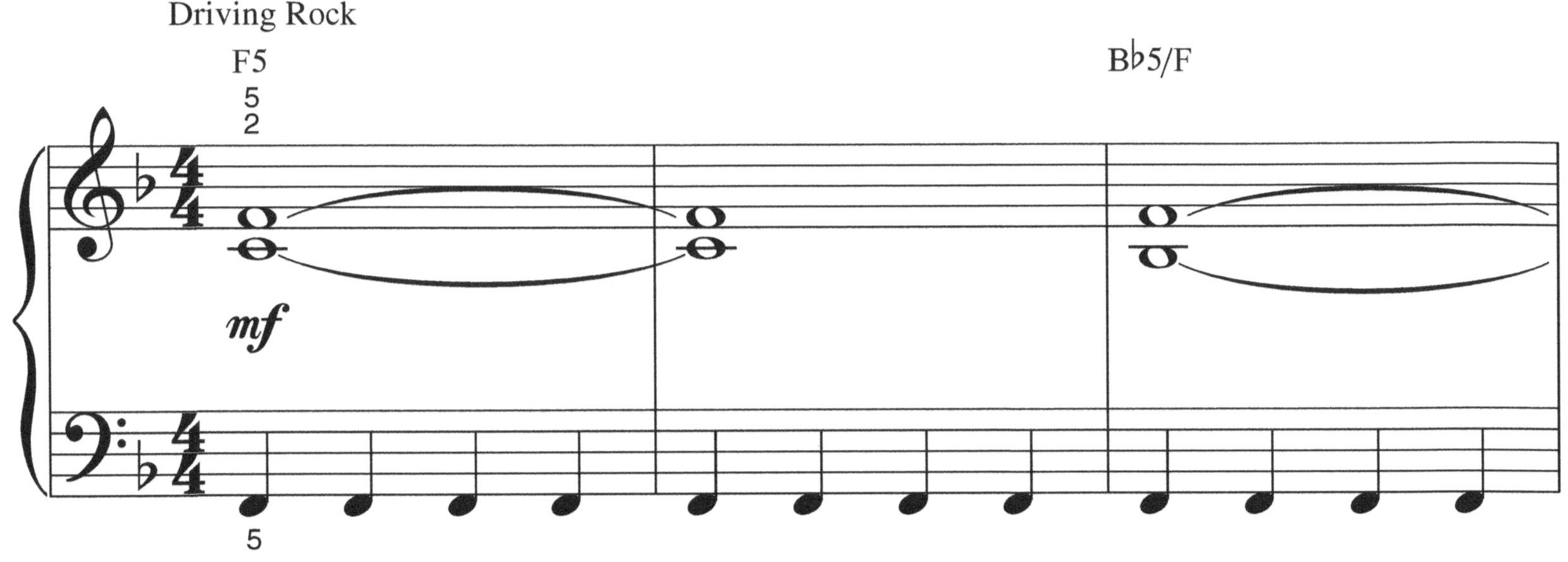

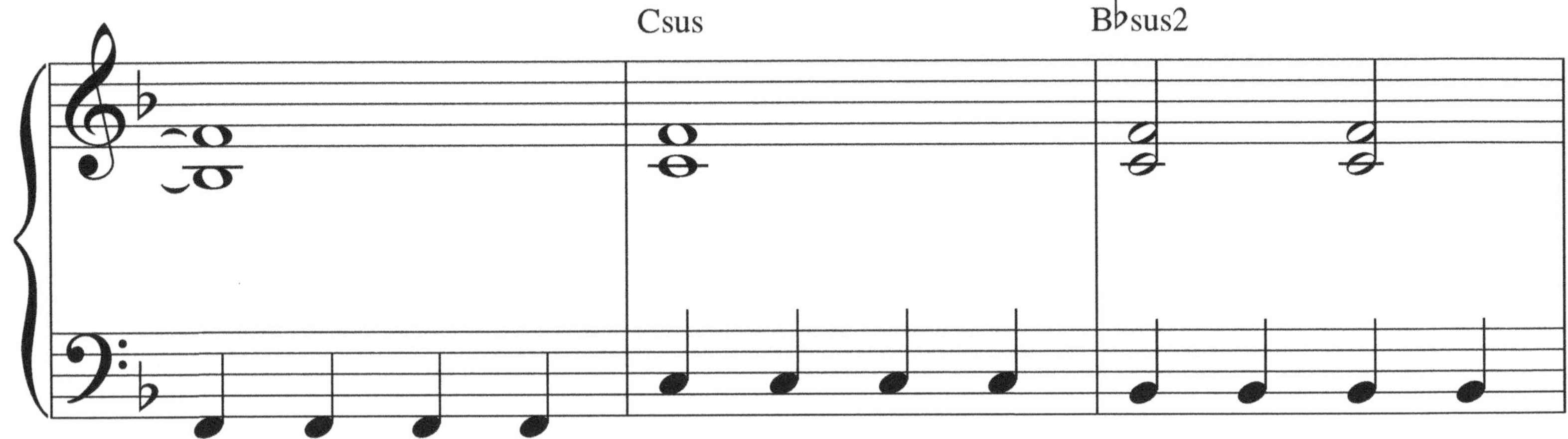

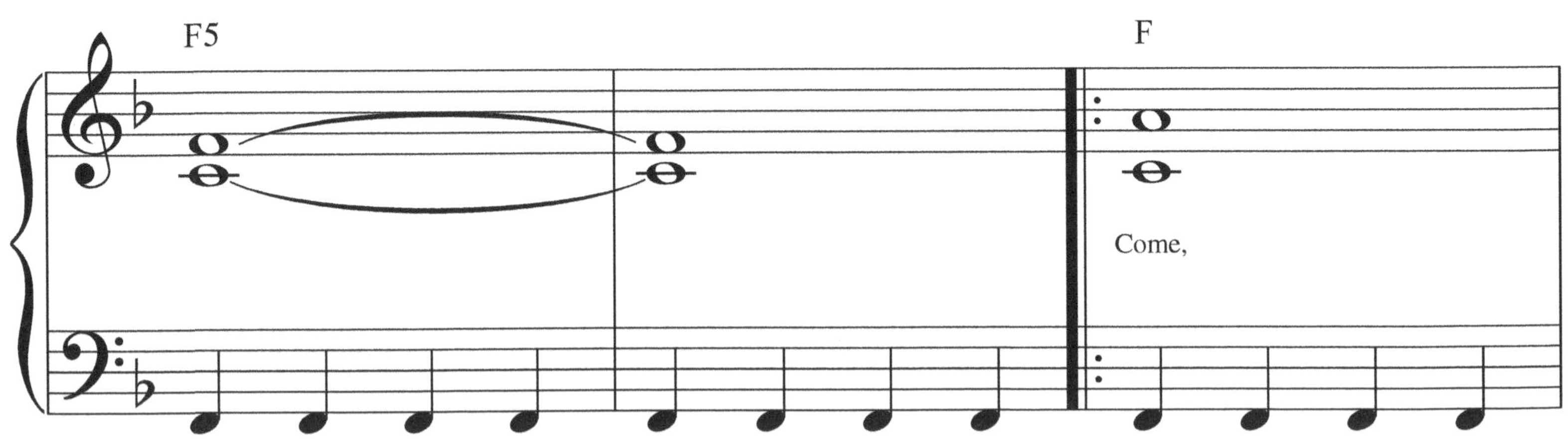

B♭/F
F
2
now is the time to wor - ship.
C5
2
Gm7
F/A
Come, now is the time to give your
B♭sus2
F
2
heart. Come, just as you are to
B♭/F
F
C5
wor - ship. Come,

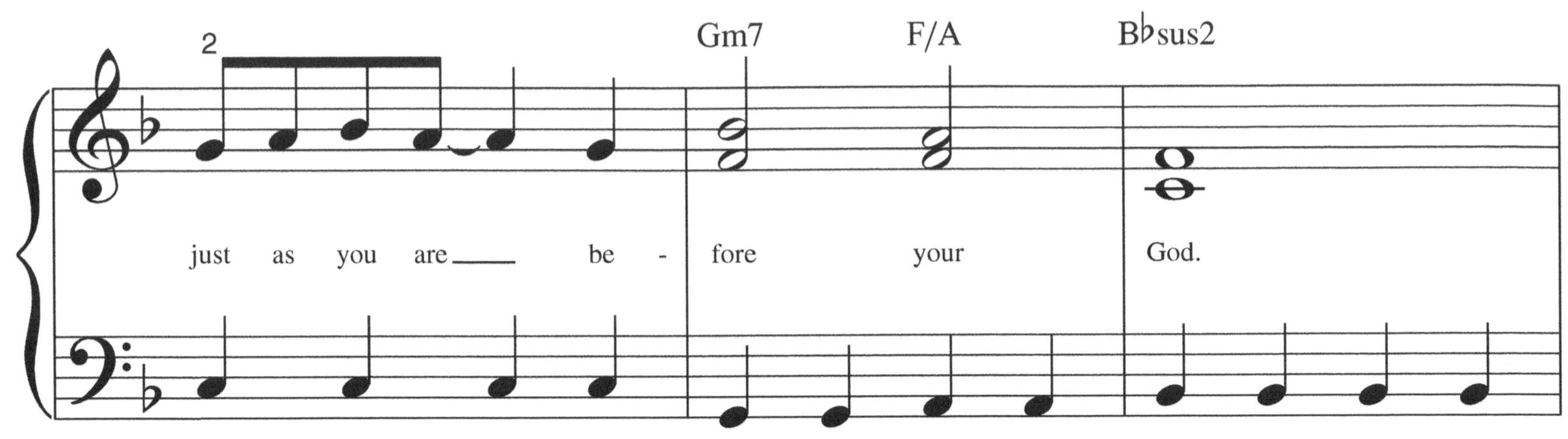
Gm7
F/A
B♭sus2
2
just as you are ___ be - fore your God.

F5
4
1
B♭
Come.
One day ev - 'ry tongue will con -

F
B♭
F
fess You are God. One day ev - 'ry knee ___ will bow.

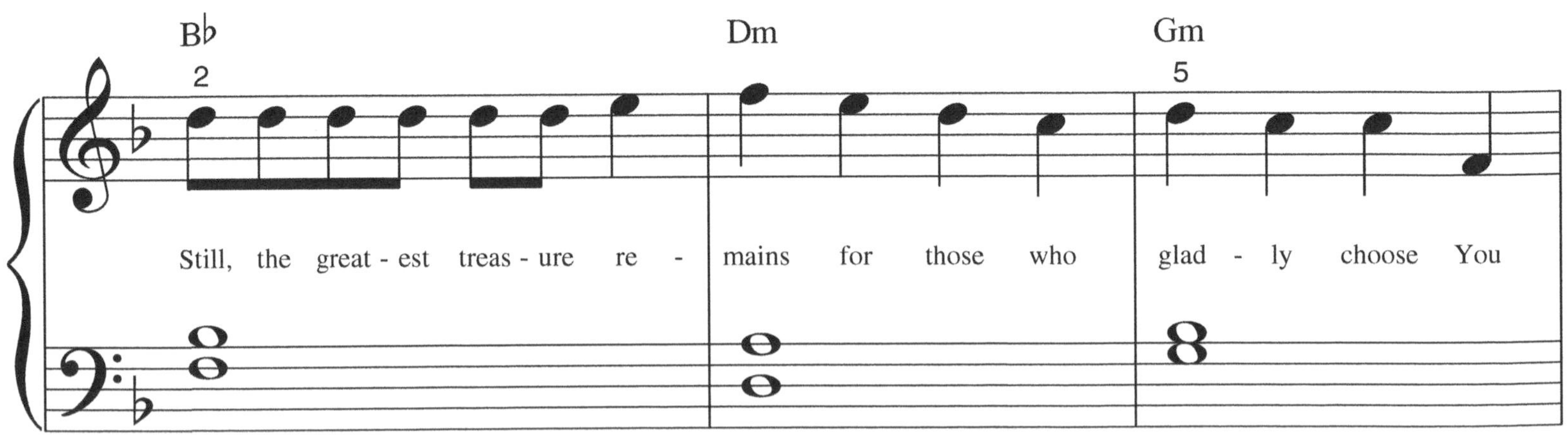
B♭
Dm
Gm
2
5
Still, the great - est treas - ure re - mains for those who glad - ly choose You

C
To Coda
1.
2.
D.S. al Coda
now.

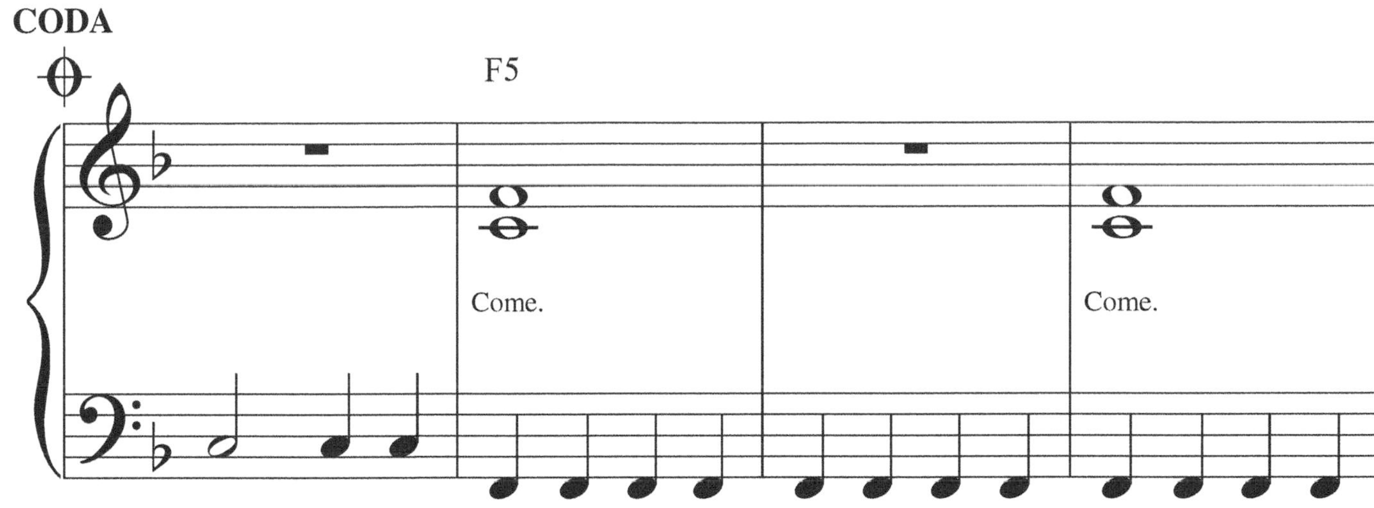
CODA
F5
Come.
Come.

Come.
Come.

FOREVER

Words and Music by
CHRIS TOMLIN

4
bove all things. His love en - dures for - ev -
been re - born, His love en - dures for - ev -
car - ry on. His love en - dures for - ev -
G
D/F♯
- er.
- er.
- er.
Sing praise, sing
1.
2., 3.
C/E
C/E
praise.
praise.
D
Sing praise, sing

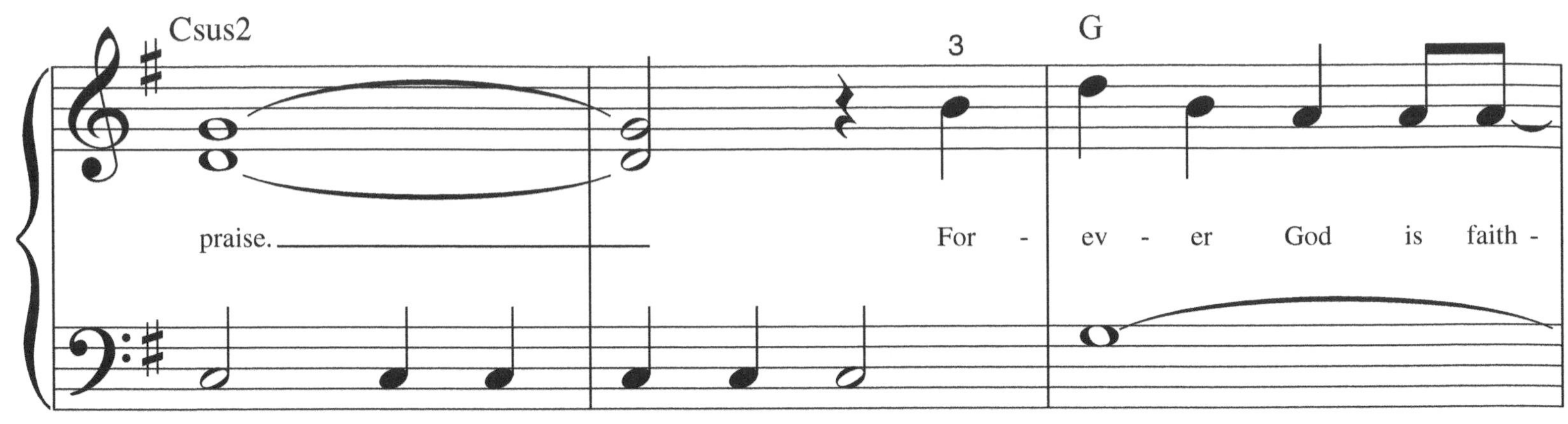
Csus2
3
G
praise.
For - ev - er God is faith -

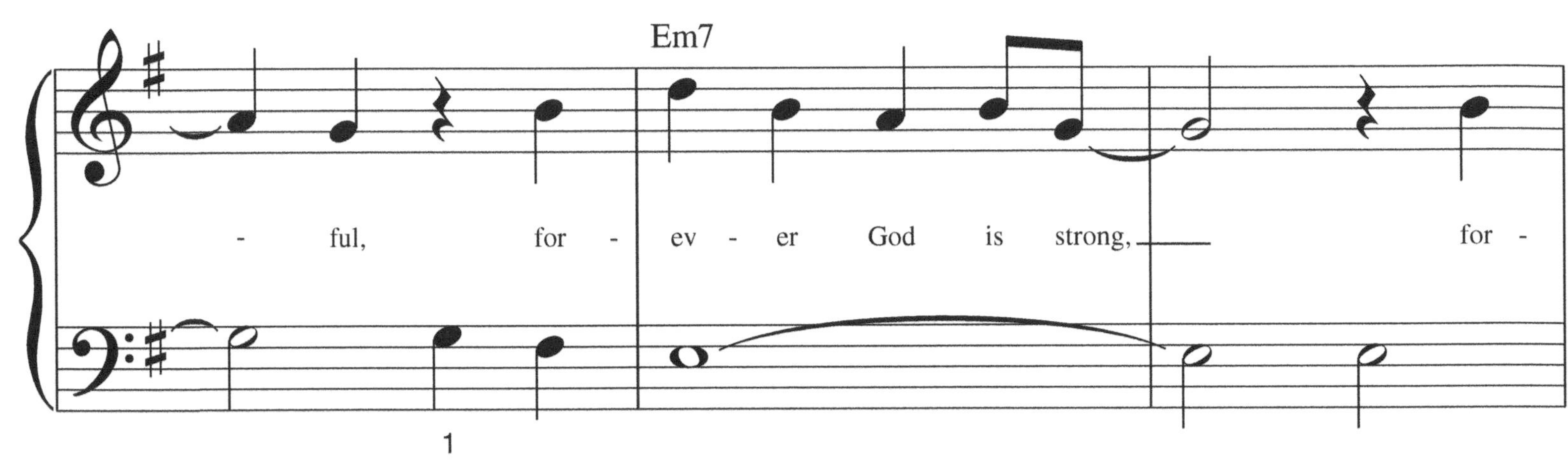
Em7
- ful, for - ev - er God is strong, for -
1

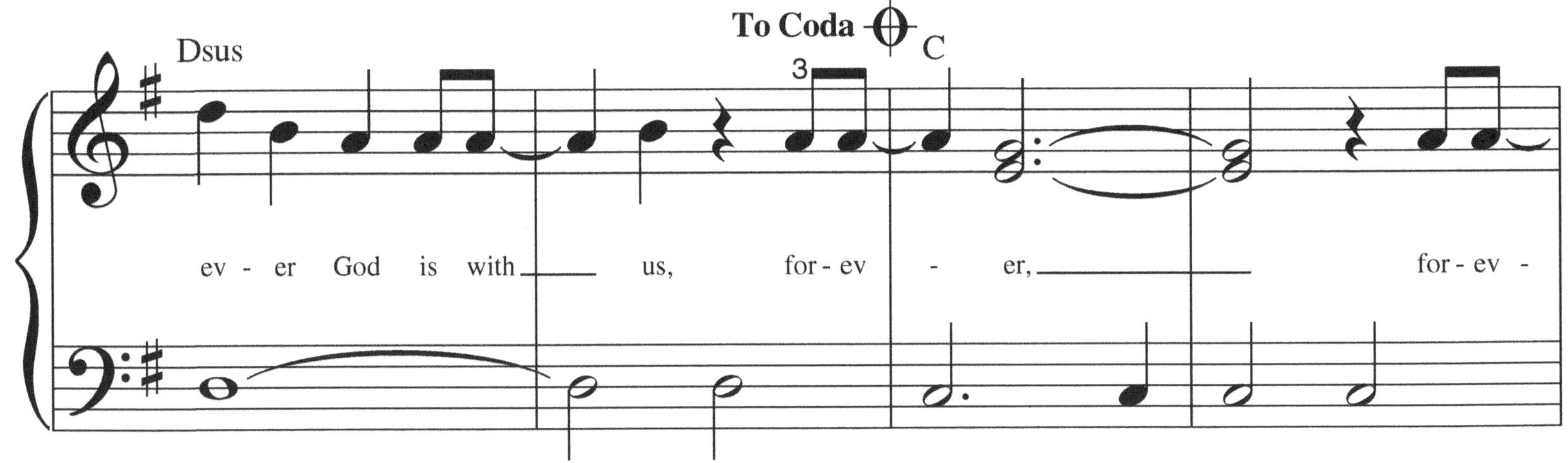
Dsus
To Coda
3
C
ev - er God is with us, for - ev - er, for - ev -

G
D.S. al Coda
(take 2nd ending)
2
- er.

CODA
C
G
3
- er and ev - er and ev - er. For -
ev - er God is faith -

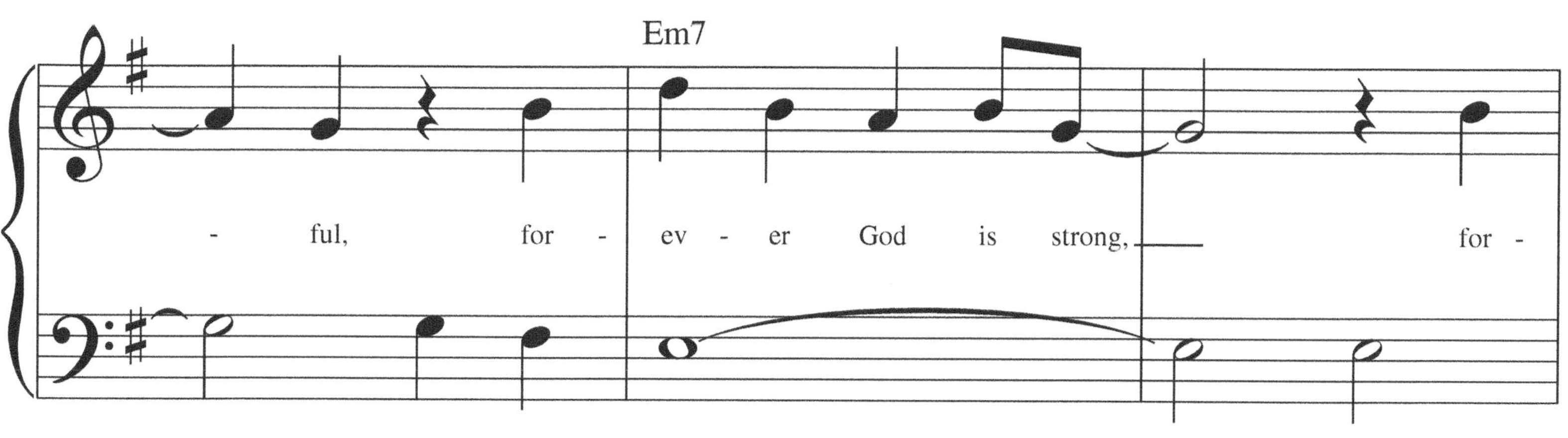
Em7
- ful, for - ev - er God is strong, for -

Dsus
3
C
ev - er God is with us, for - ev - er, for - ev -

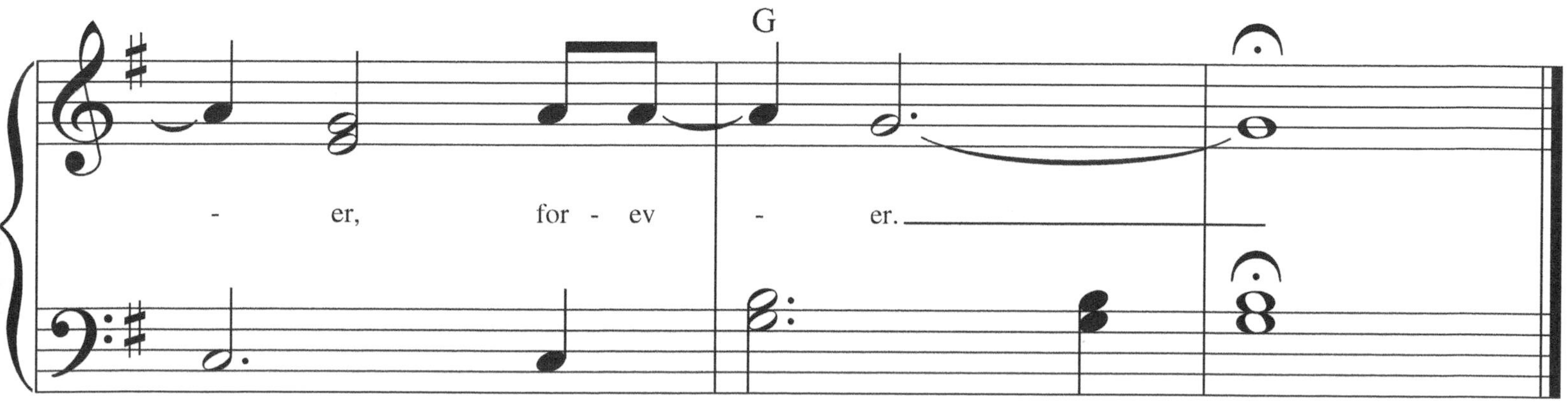
G
- er, for - ev - er.

GREAT IS THE LORD

Words and Music by MICHAEL W. SMITH
and DEBORAH D. SMITH

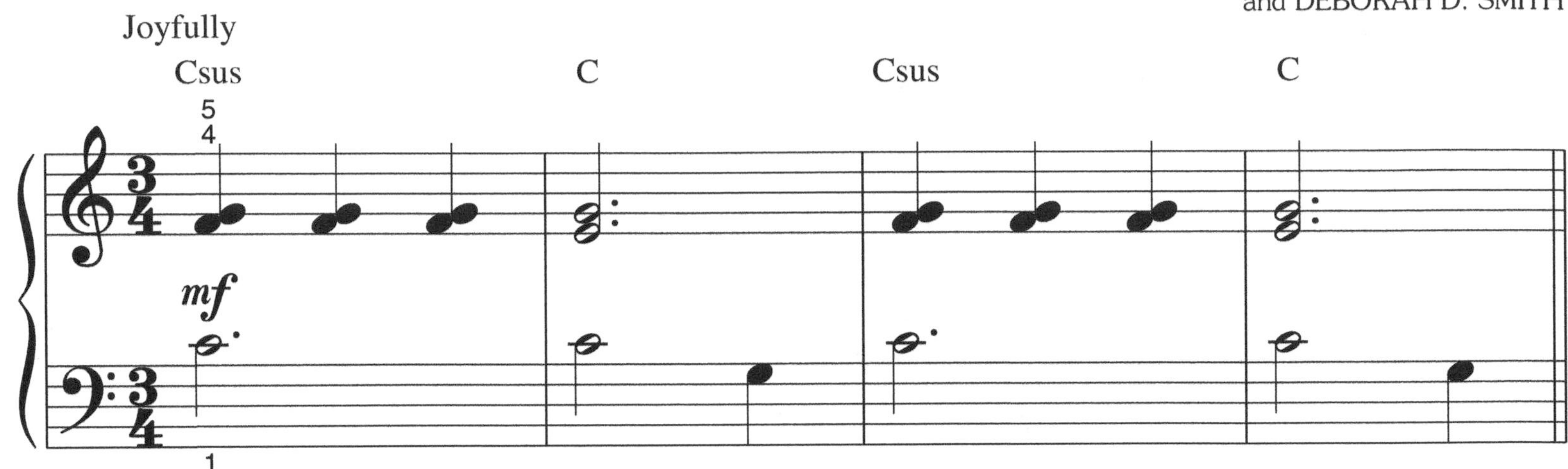

F/A
G/B
F
C
1
5
mer - cy He
proves He is
love.
2

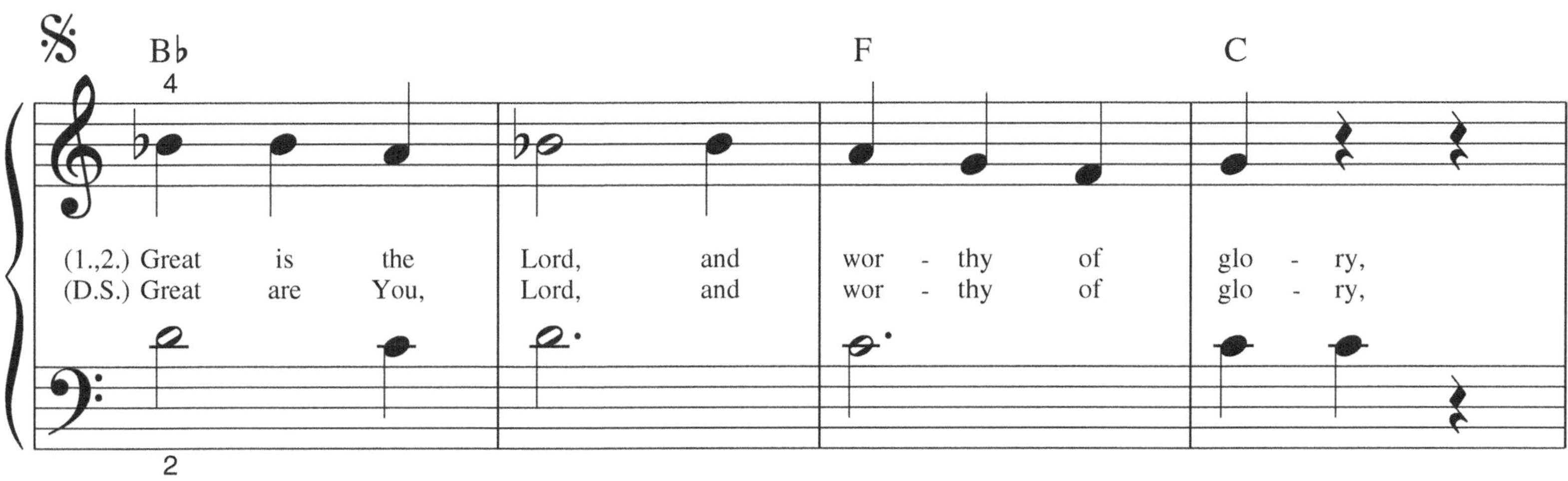
B♭
F
C
4
(1.,2.) Great is the
(D.S.) Great are You,
Lord, and
Lord, and
wor - thy of
wor - thy of
glo - ry,
glo - ry,
2

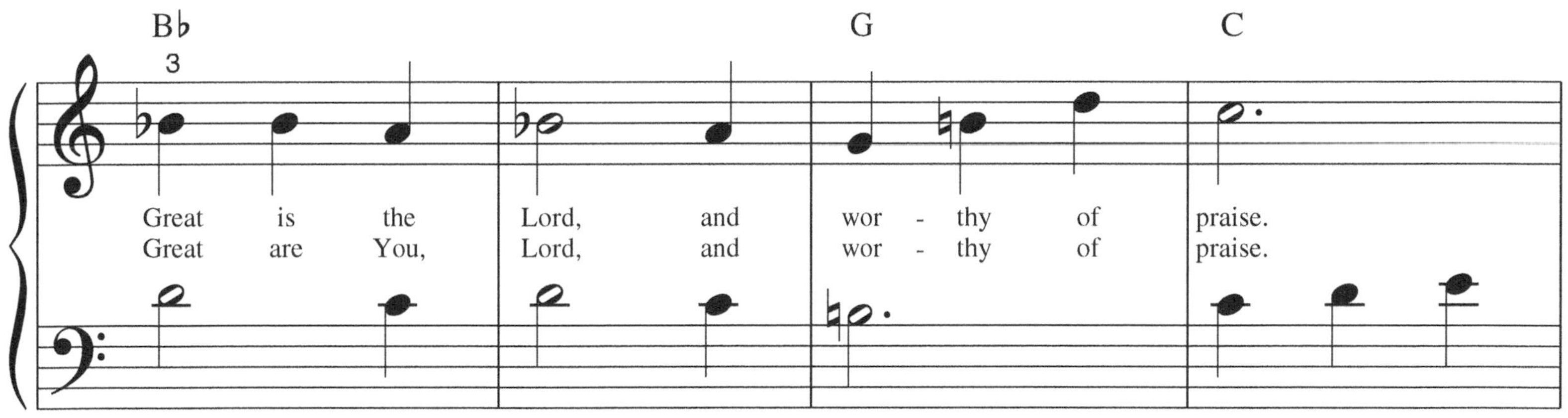
B♭
G
C
3
Great is the
Great are You,
Lord, and
Lord, and
wor - thy of
wor - thy of
praise.
praise.

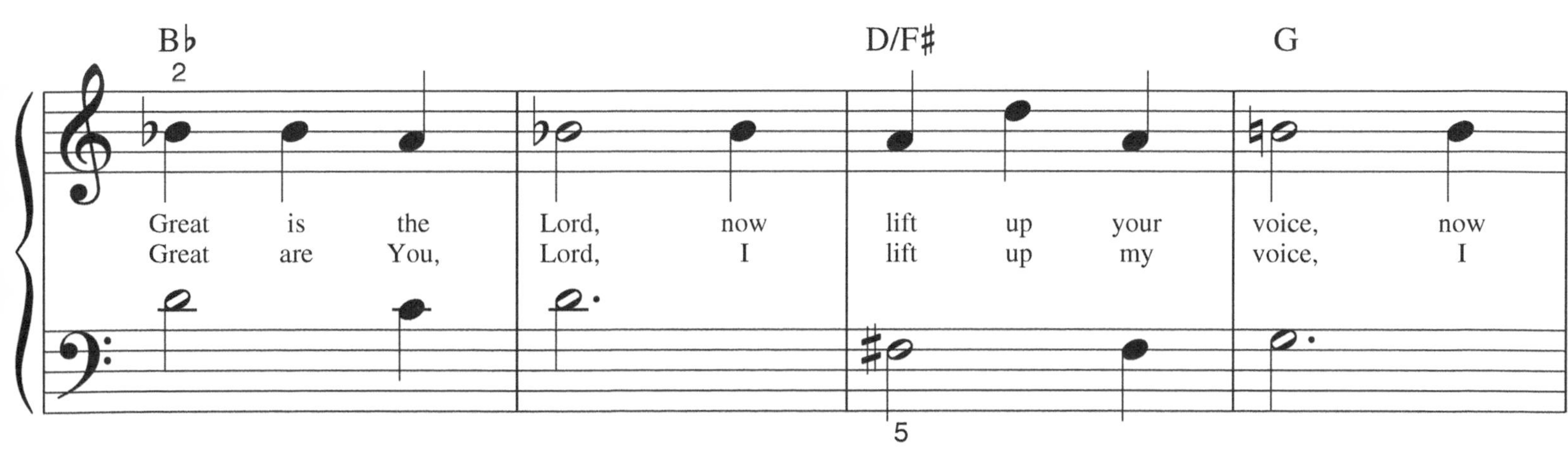
B♭
D/F♯
G
2
Great is the
Great are You,
Lord, now
Lord, I
lift up your
lift up my
voice, now
voice, I
5

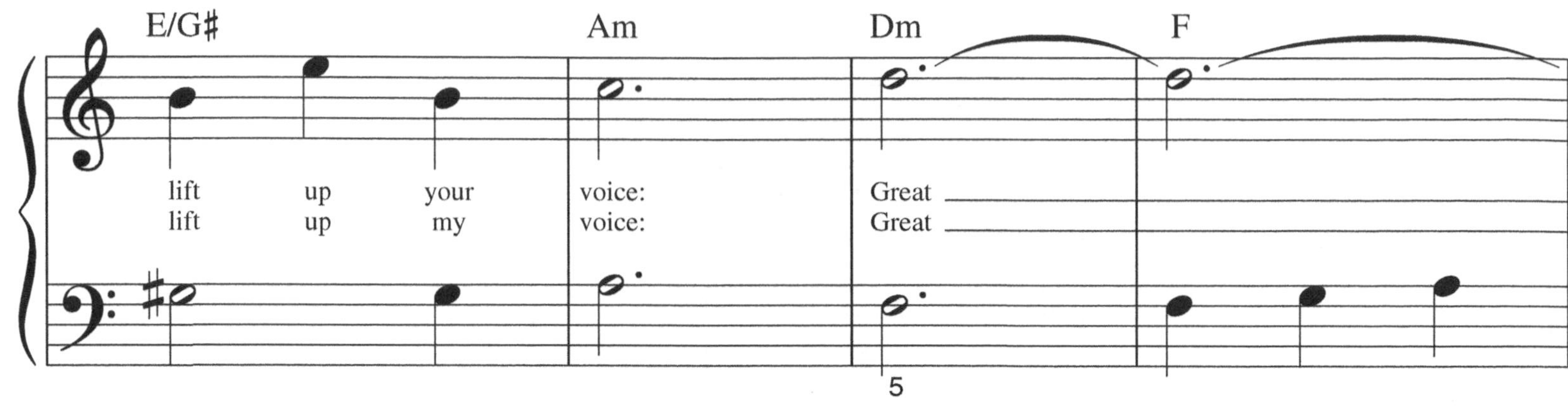
E/G#
Am
Dm
F
lift up your voice: Great
lift up my voice: Great
5

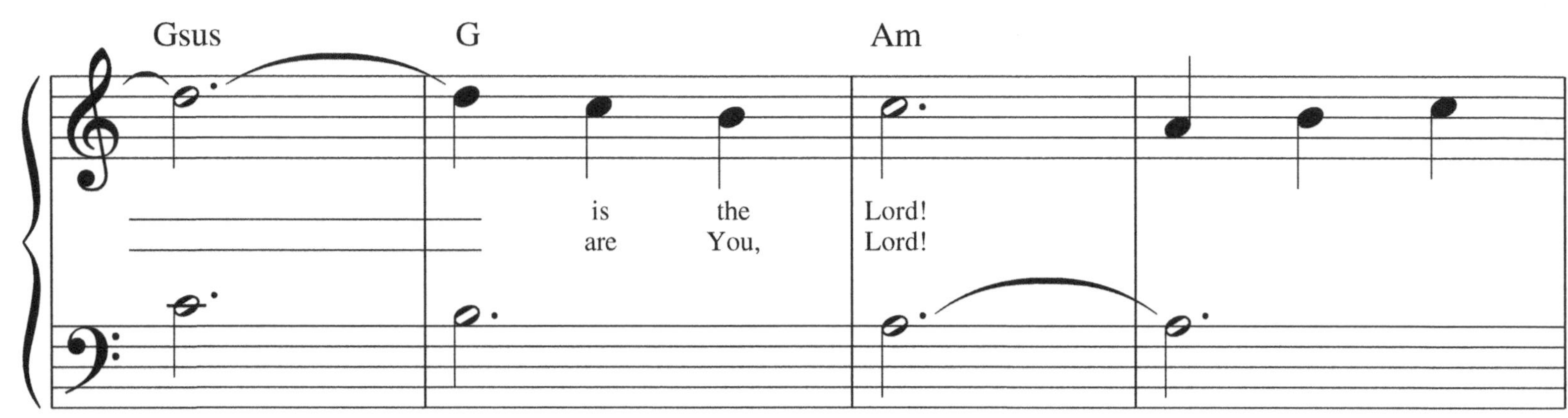
Gsus
G
Am
is the Lord!
are You, Lord!

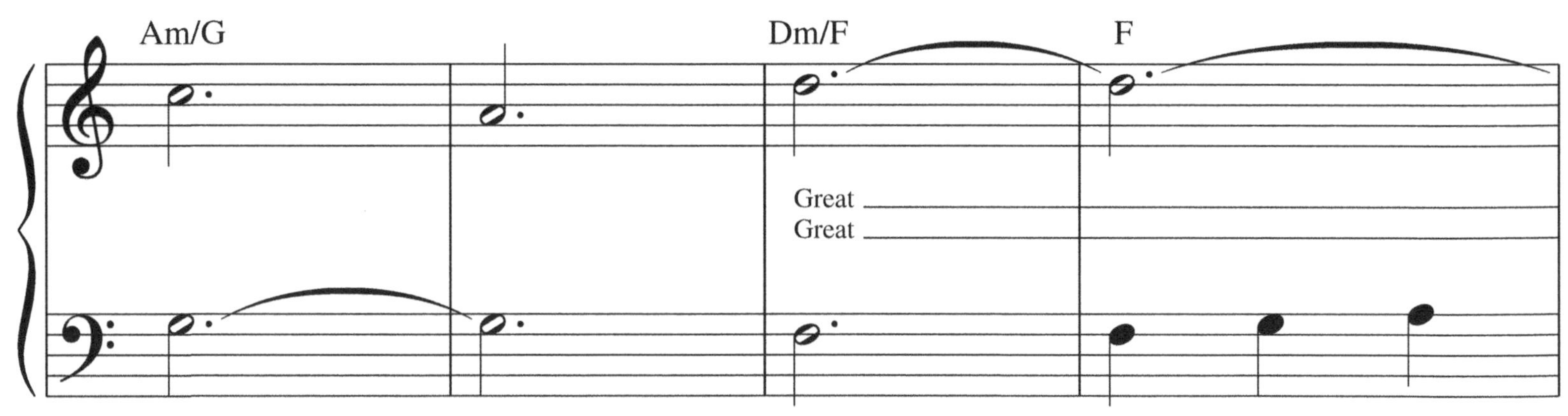
Am/G
Dm/F
F
Great
Great

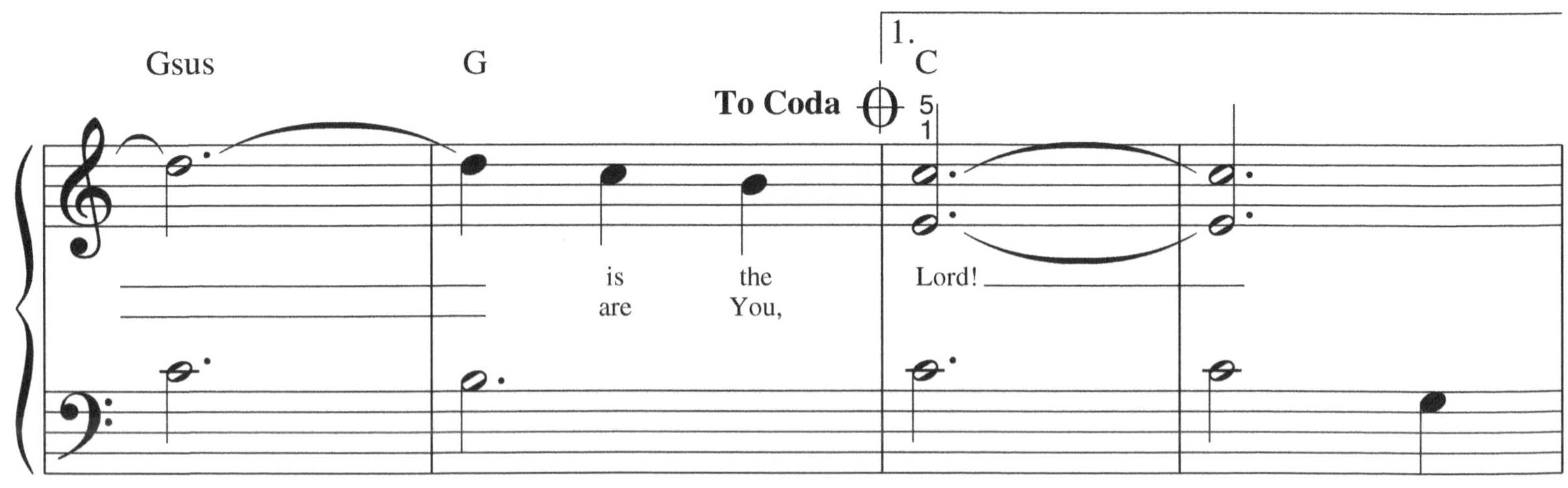
Gsus
G
1.
C
To Coda
5
1
is the Lord!
are You,

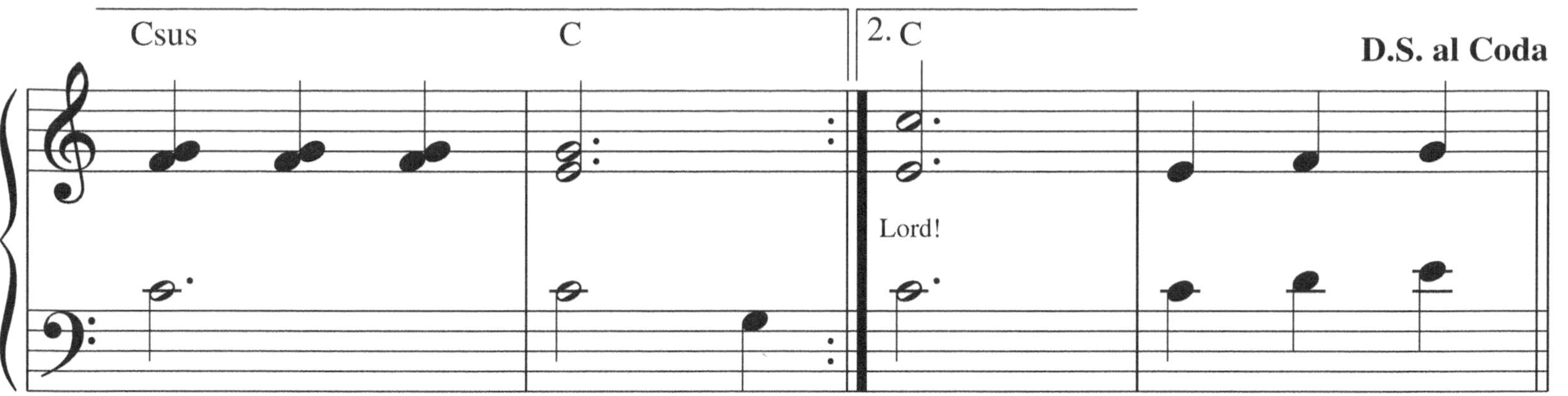
Csus
C
2. C
D.S. al Coda
Lord!

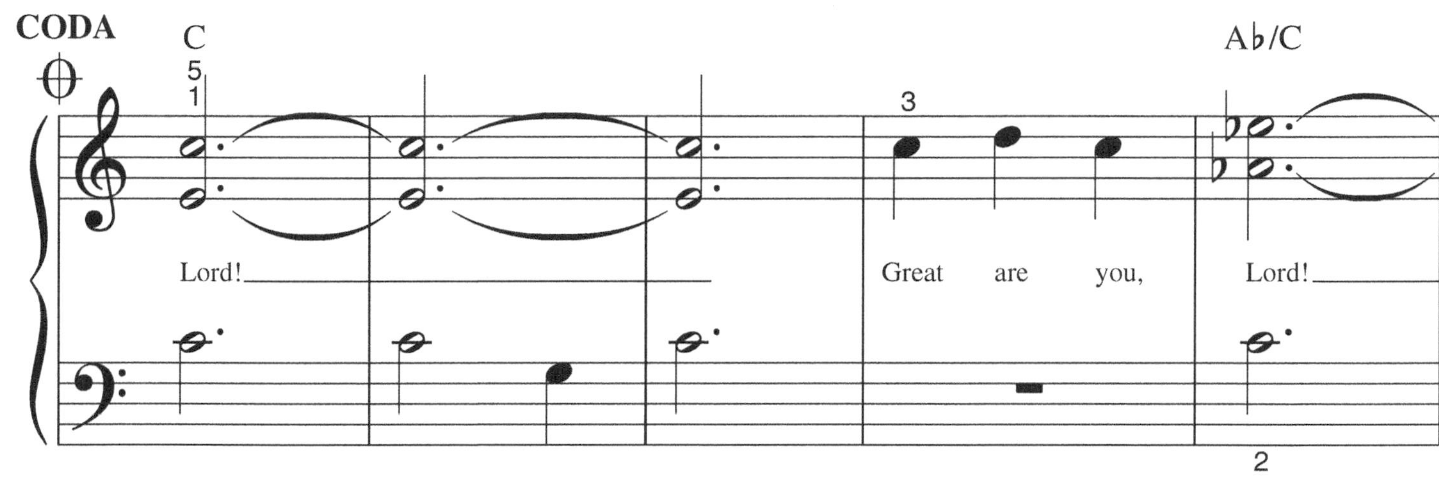
CODA
C
A♭/C
Lord!
Great are you,
Lord!

B♭/D
Great are you,
Lord!

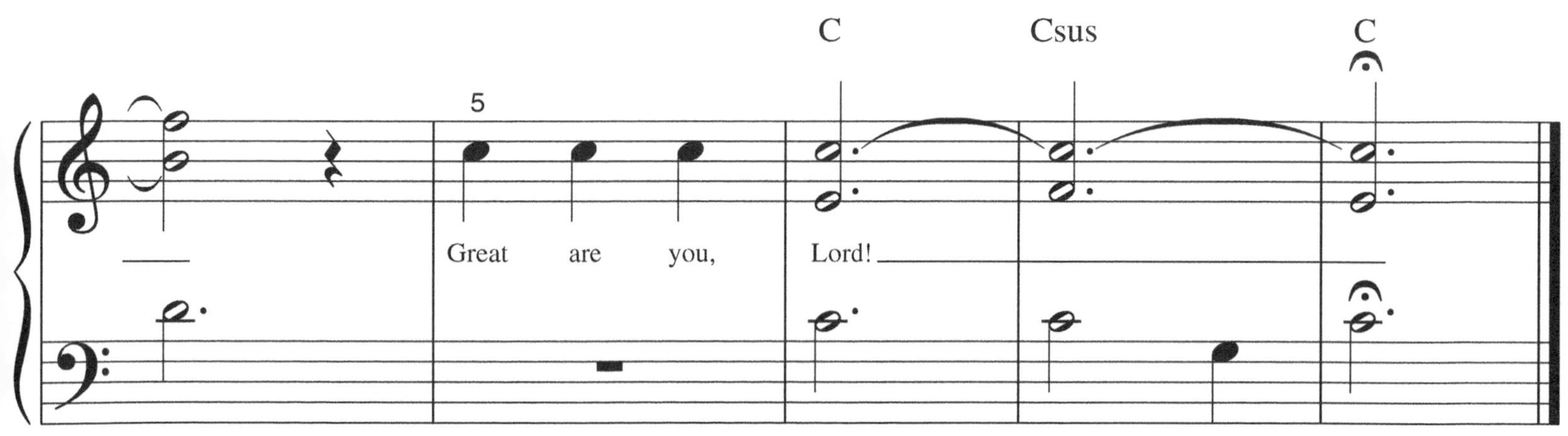
C
Csus
C
Great are you,
Lord!

HE IS EXALTED

Words and Music by
TWILA PARIS

C C/E

high; I will praise

D/F♯ G

Him. He is ex - alt - ed, for -

5

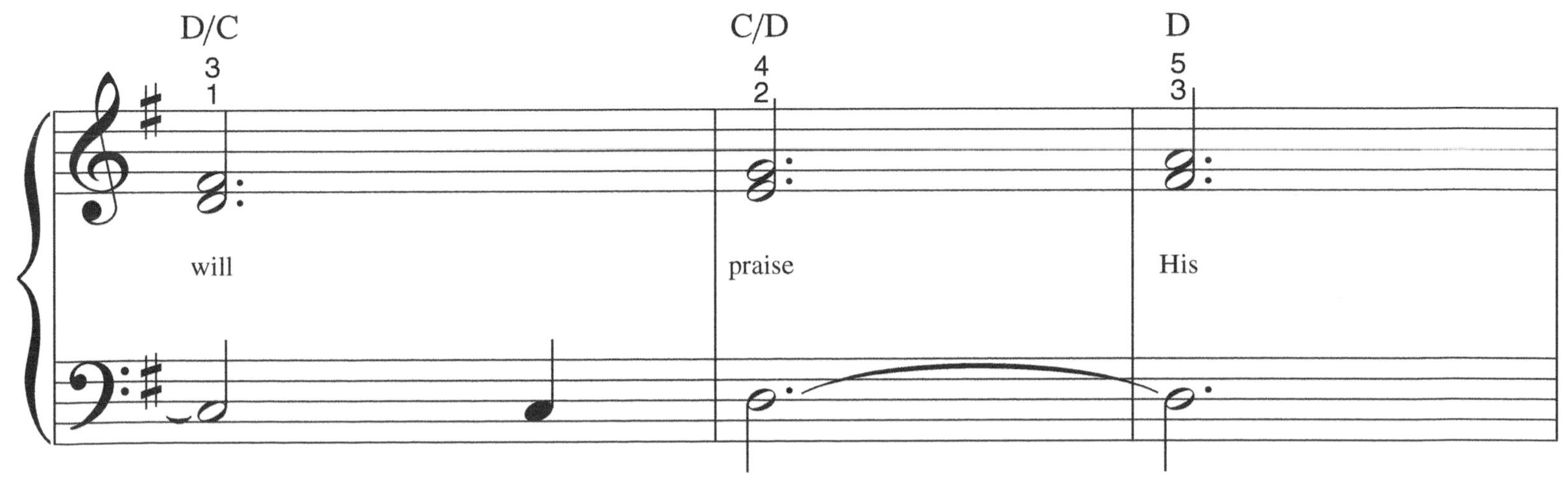

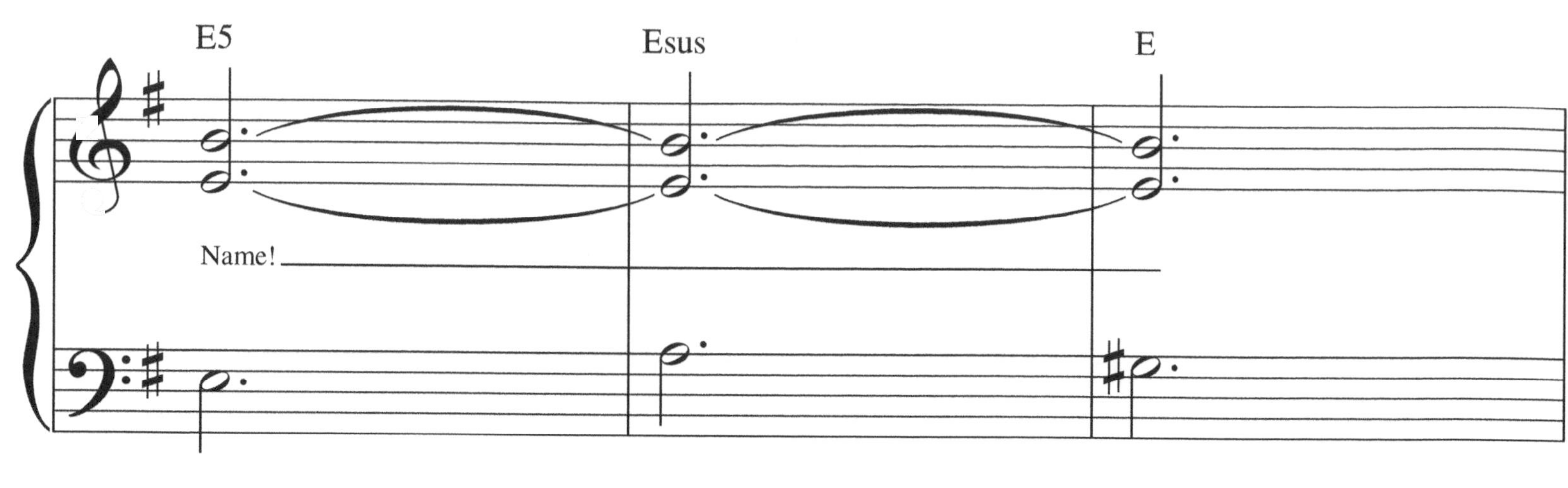
E5
Esus
E
Name!

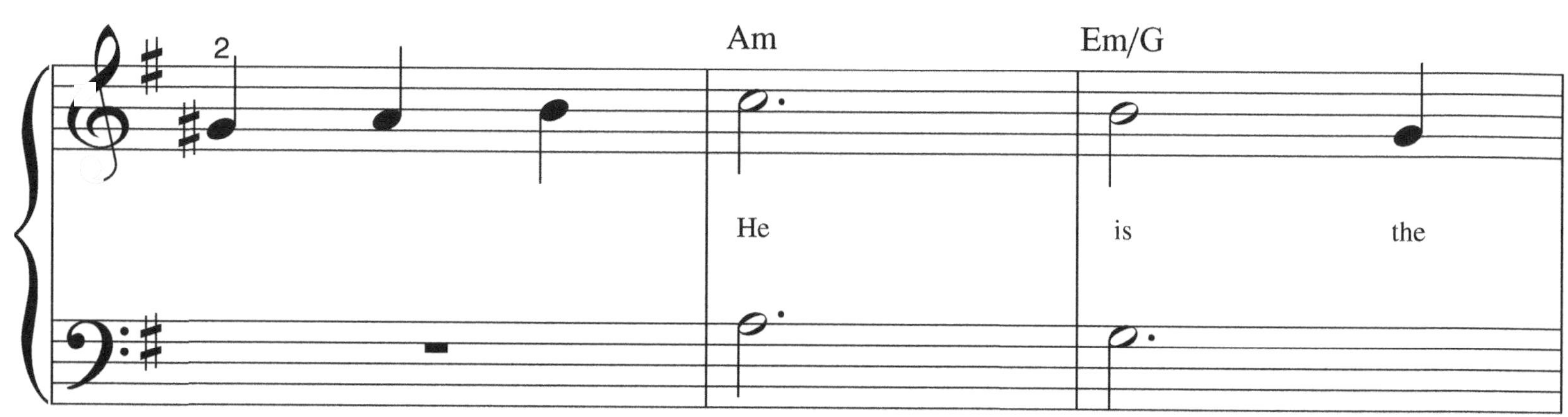
2
Am
Em/G
He
is
the

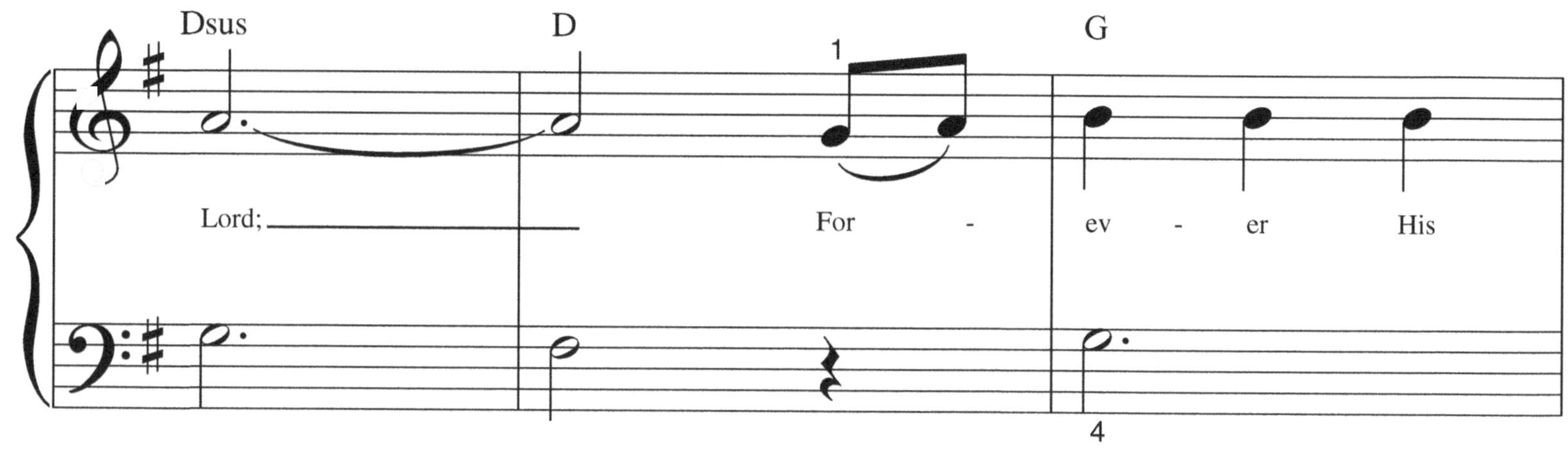
Dsus
D
1
G
Lord;
For
-
ev
-
er
His
4

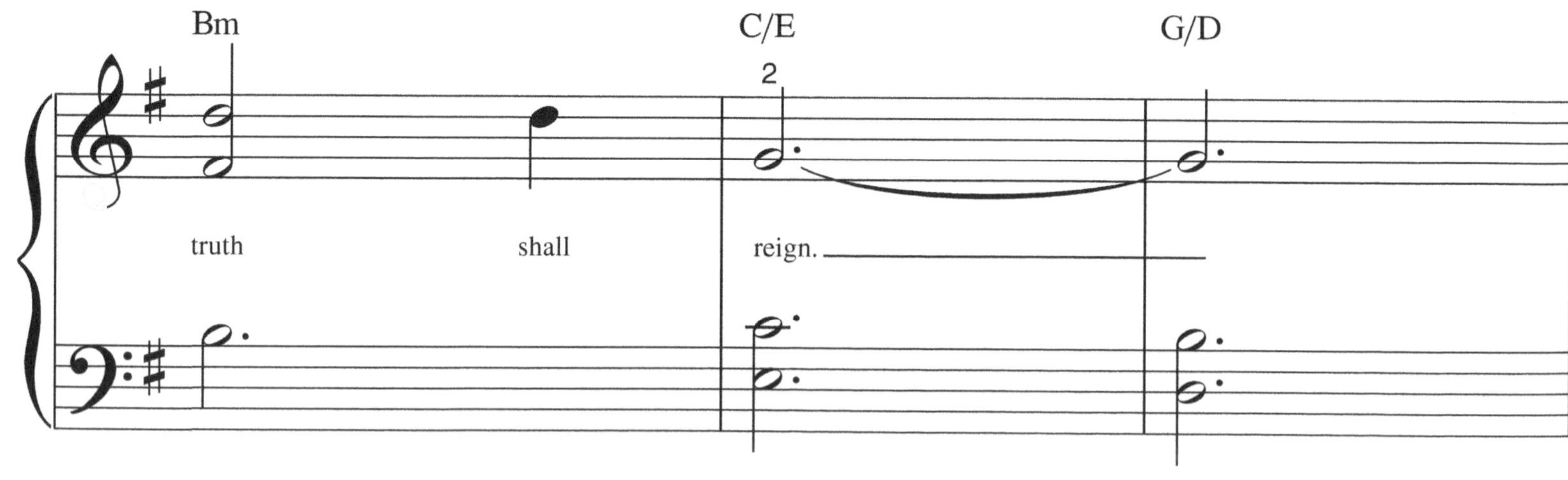
Bm
C/E
2
G/D
truth
shall
reign.

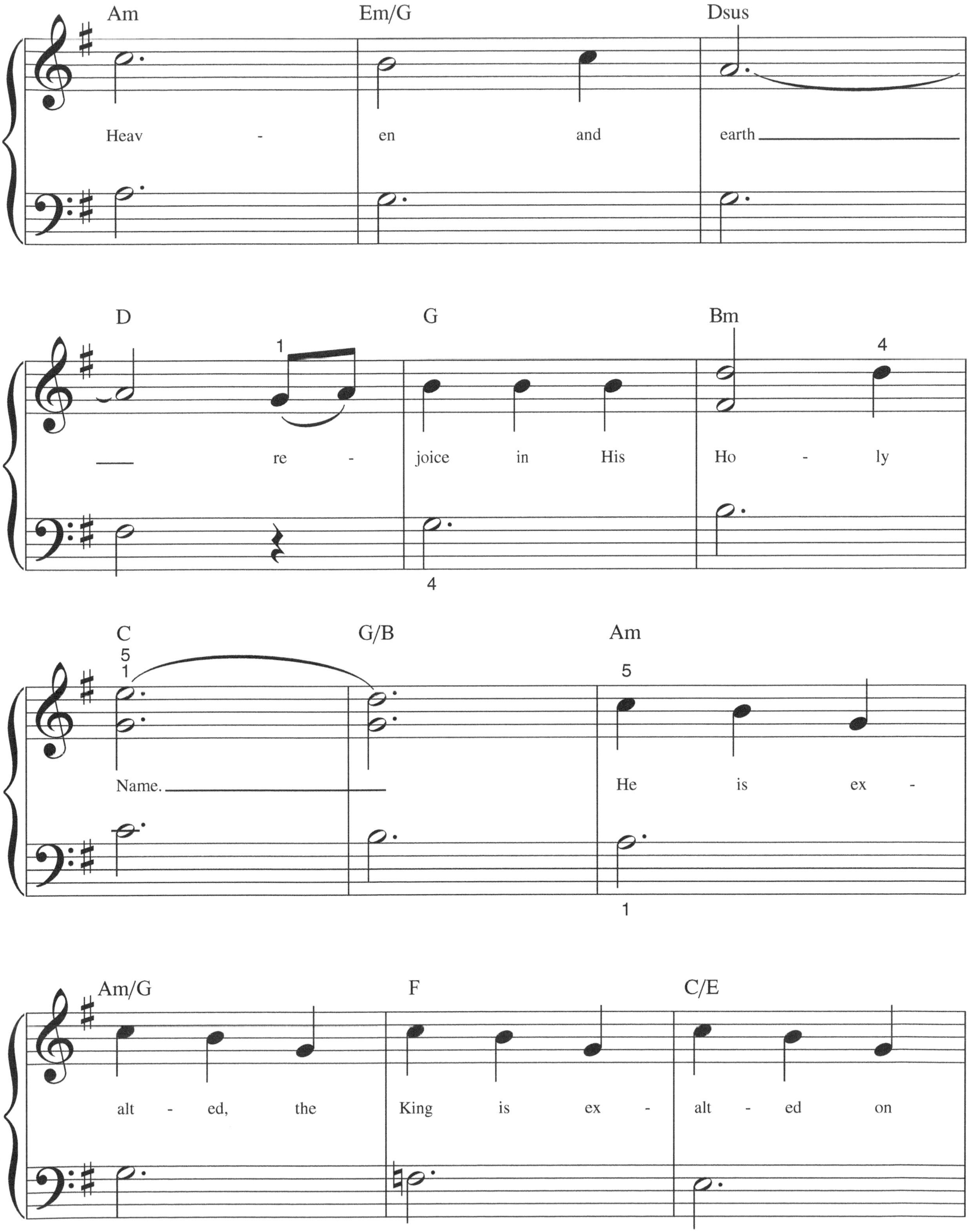

Am
Em/G
Dsus
Heav - en and earth
D
G
Bm
1
4
re - joice in His Ho - ly
4
C
G/B
Am
5
1
5
Name. He is ex -
1
Am/G
F
C/E
alt - ed, the King is ex - alt - ed on

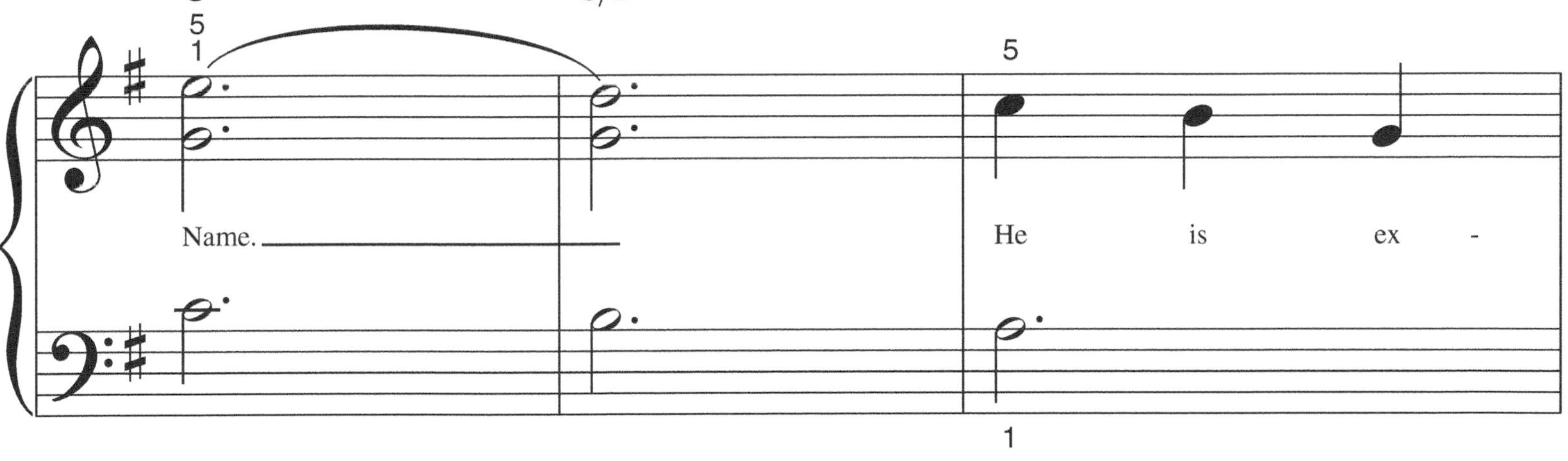

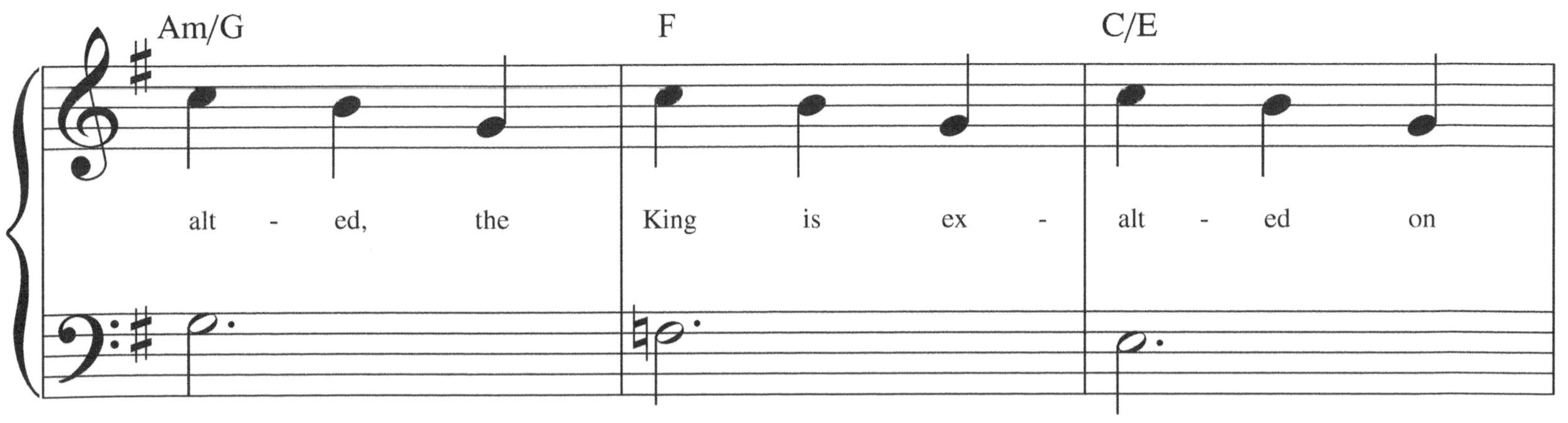

G
Esus
high.

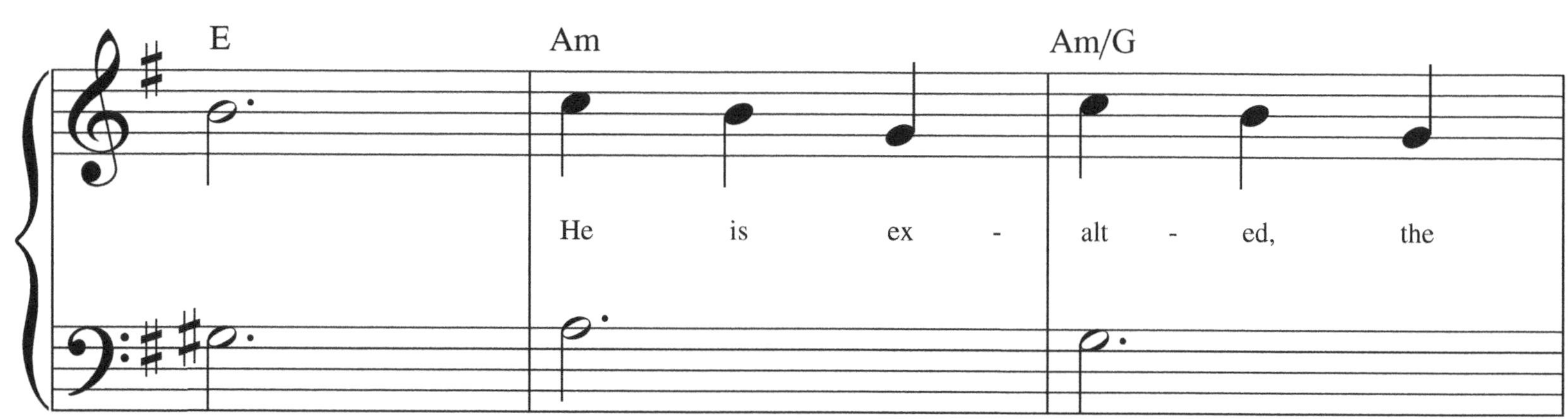
E
Am
Am/G
He is ex - alt - ed, the

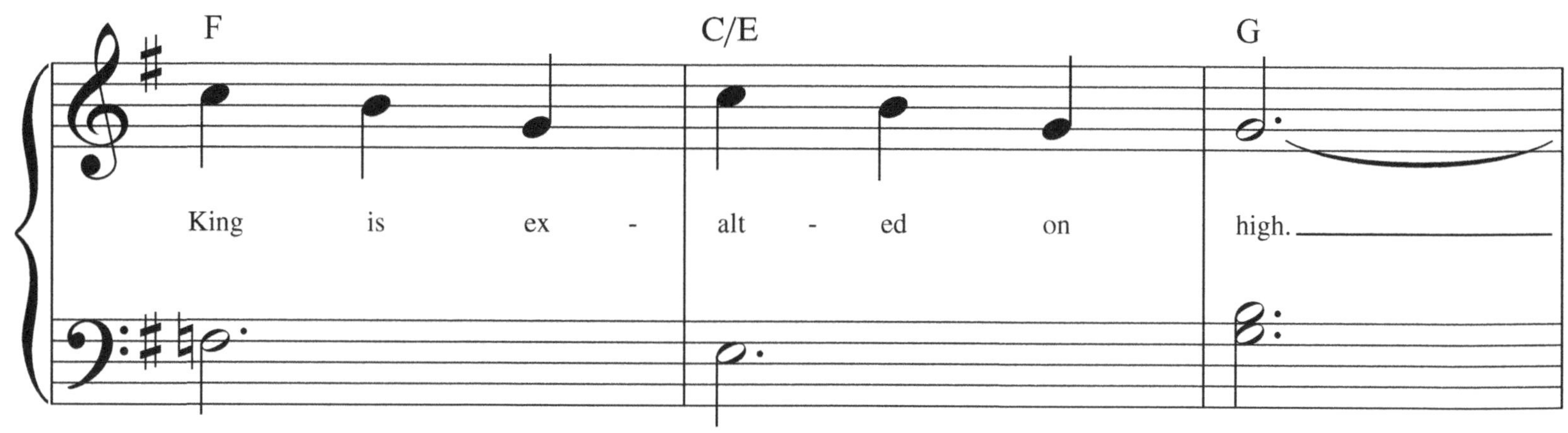
F
C/E
G
King is ex - alt - ed on high.

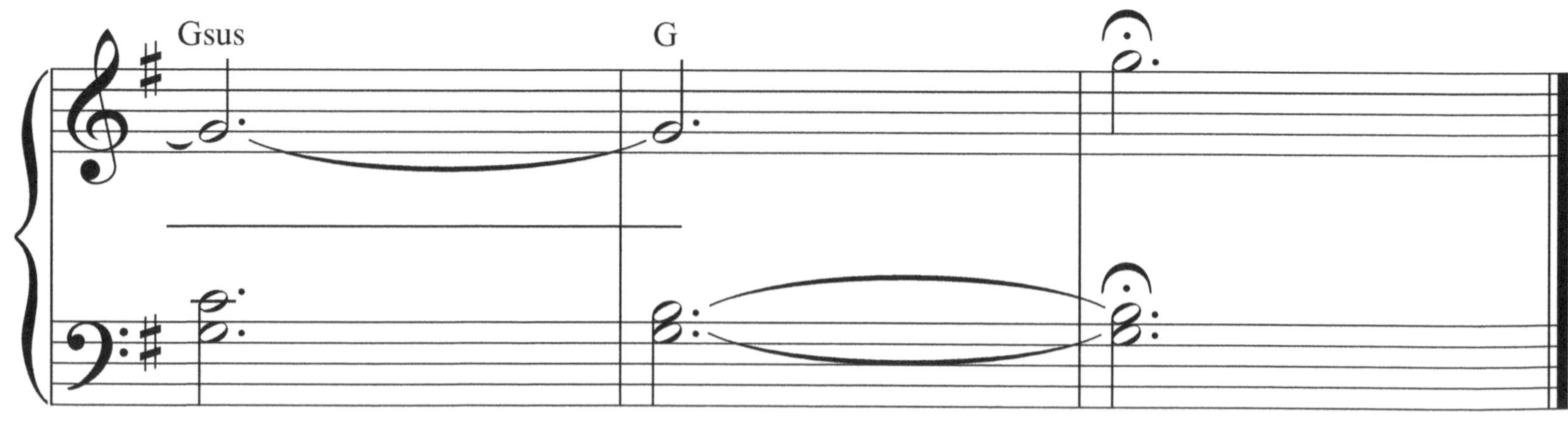
Gsus
G

HERE I AM TO WORSHIP

Words and Music by
TIM HUGHES

Moderately slow

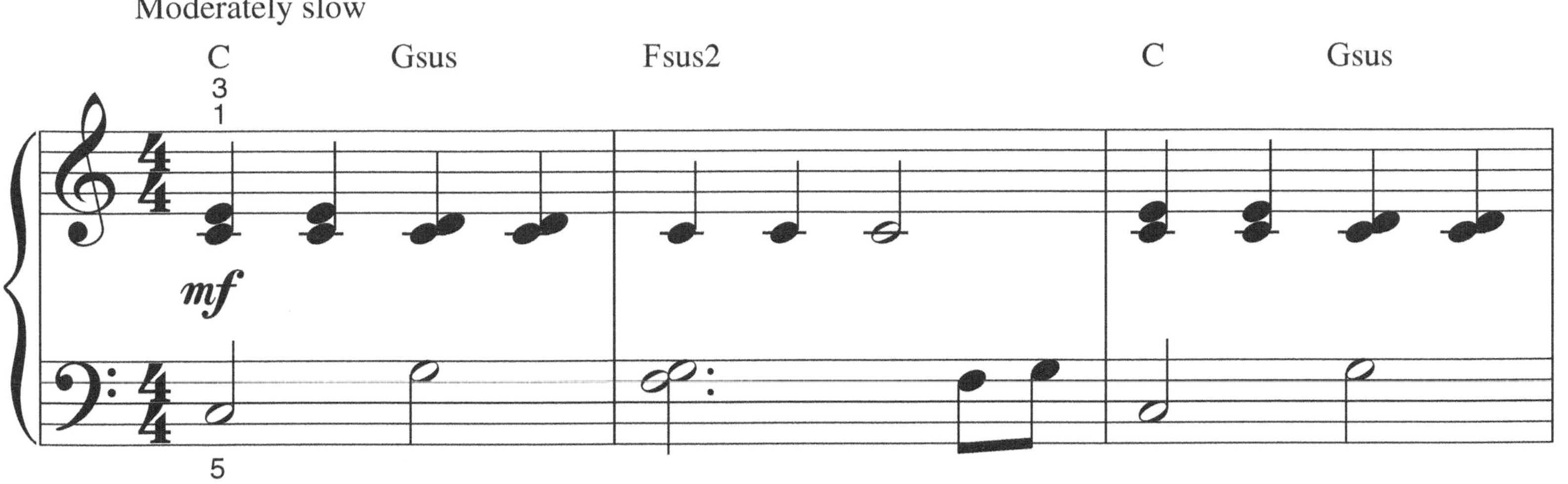

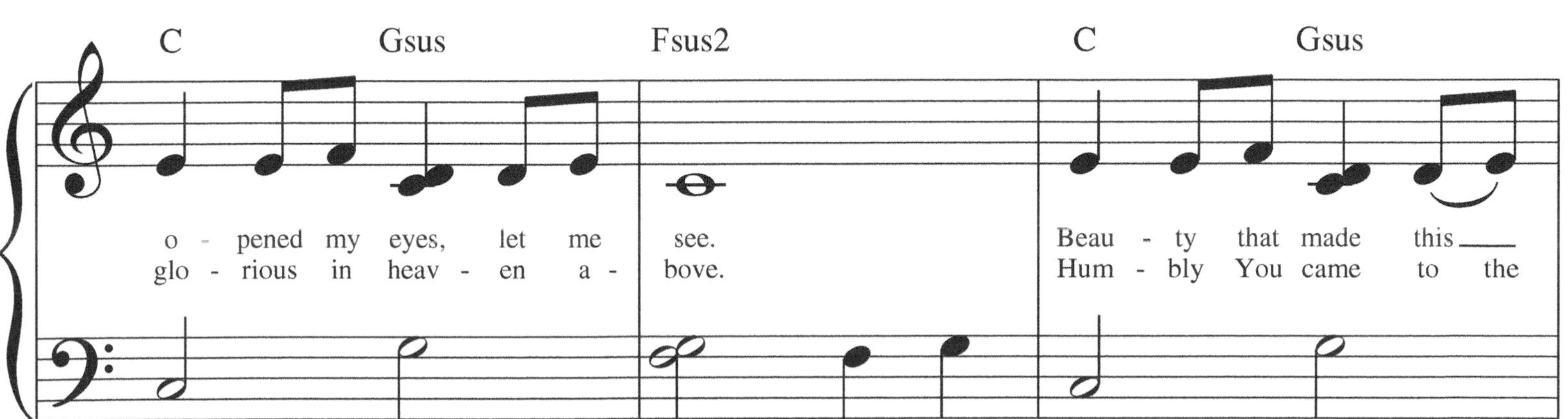

Dm
C
Gsus
heart a - dore You,
earth You cre - a - ted,
hope of a life spent with
all for love's sake be - came

Fsus2
F
C
4
You.
poor.
Here I am to
wor - ship, here I am to

G/B
C
Fsus2
bow down, here I am to
say that You're my God.
You're al - to - geth - er

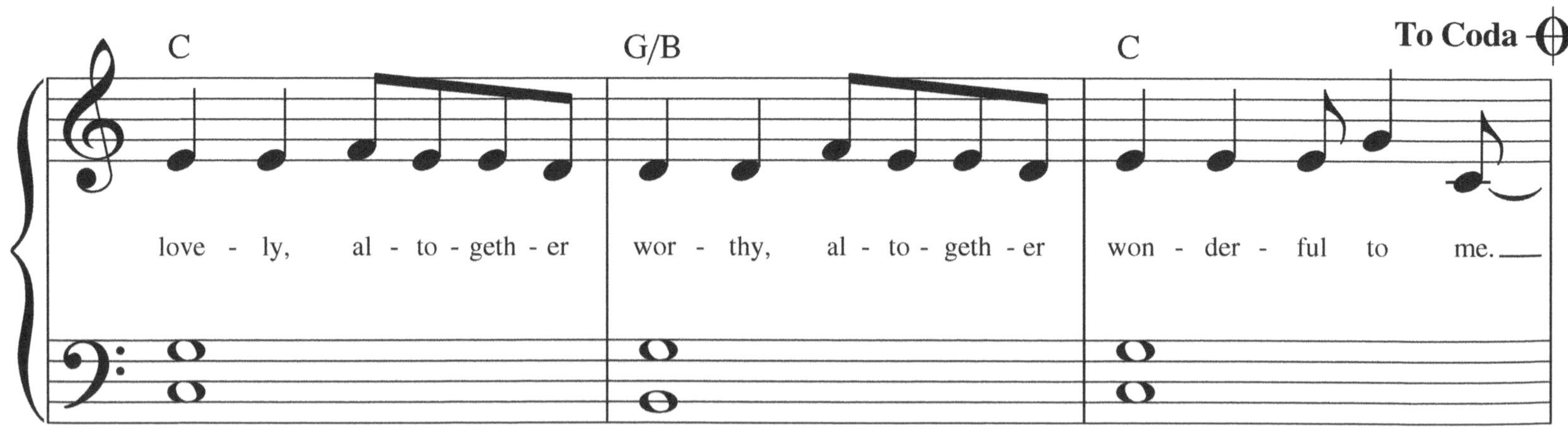
C
G/B
C
To Coda
love - ly, al - to - geth - er
wor - thy, al - to - geth - er
won - der - ful to me.

1.
Fsus2
2.
Fsus2
And I'll nev -
G/B C F/C G/B C
- er know how much it cost to see my sin up -
1.
F/C
on that cross. And I'll nev -
2.
F/C G/B
D.S. al Coda
on that cross. Here I am to
CODA
Fsus2 C

THE HEART OF WORSHIP

Words and Music by
MATT REDMAN

Gm7
Csus
way, and I sim - ply come,
press how much You de - serve.
C
F
long - ing just to bring
Though I'm weak and poor,
C/E
Gm7
some - thing that's of worth that will
all I have is Yours, ev - 'ry
Csus
C
bless Your heart.
sin - gle breath.

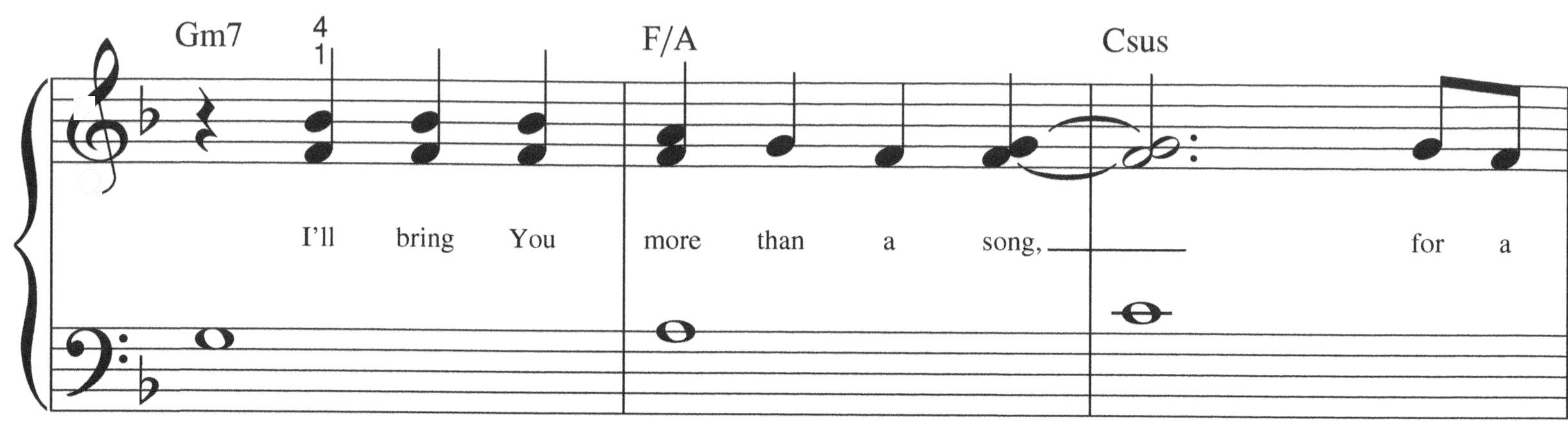
Gm7
4
1
F/A
Csus
I'll bring You more than a song, for a

Gm7
F/A
song in it - self is not what You have re - quired.
1
4

Csus
C
Gm7
You search much

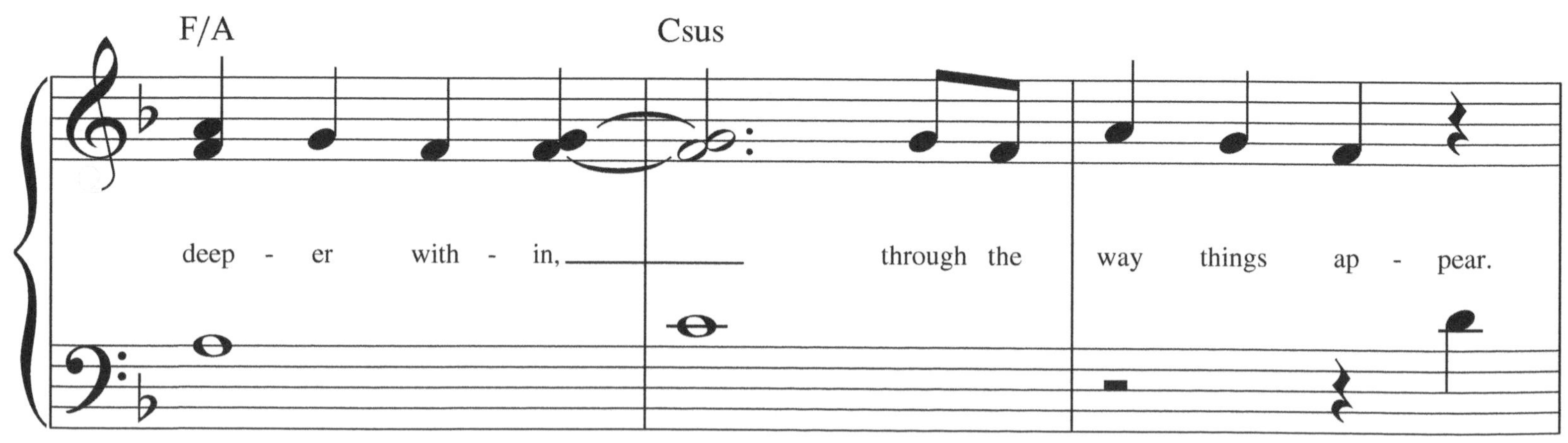
F/A
Csus
deep - er with - in, through the way things ap - pear.

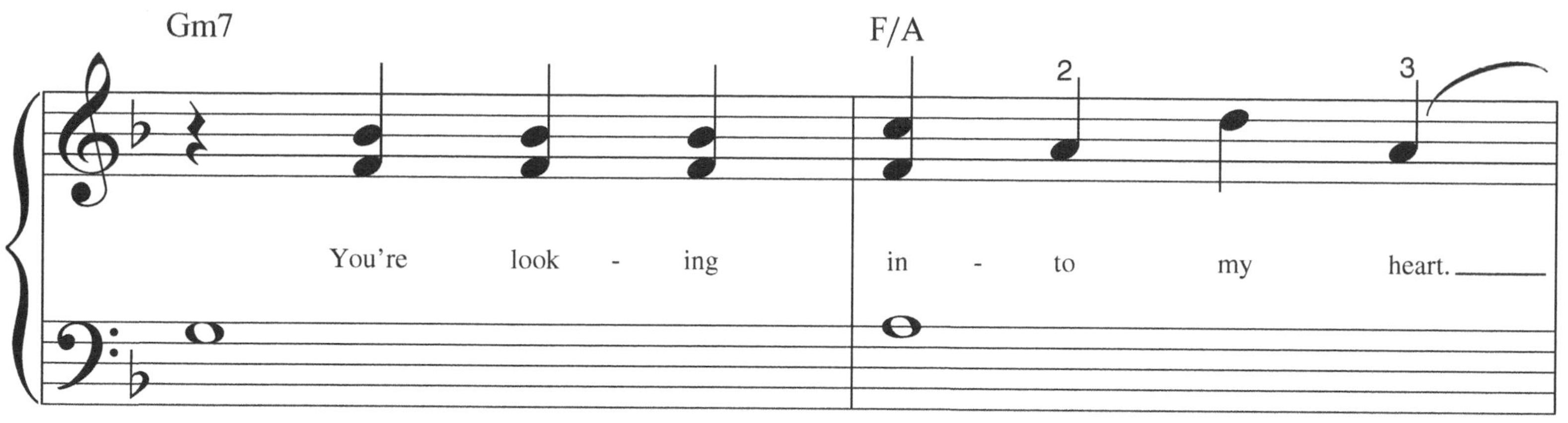
Gm7
F/A
2
3
You're look - ing in - to my heart.

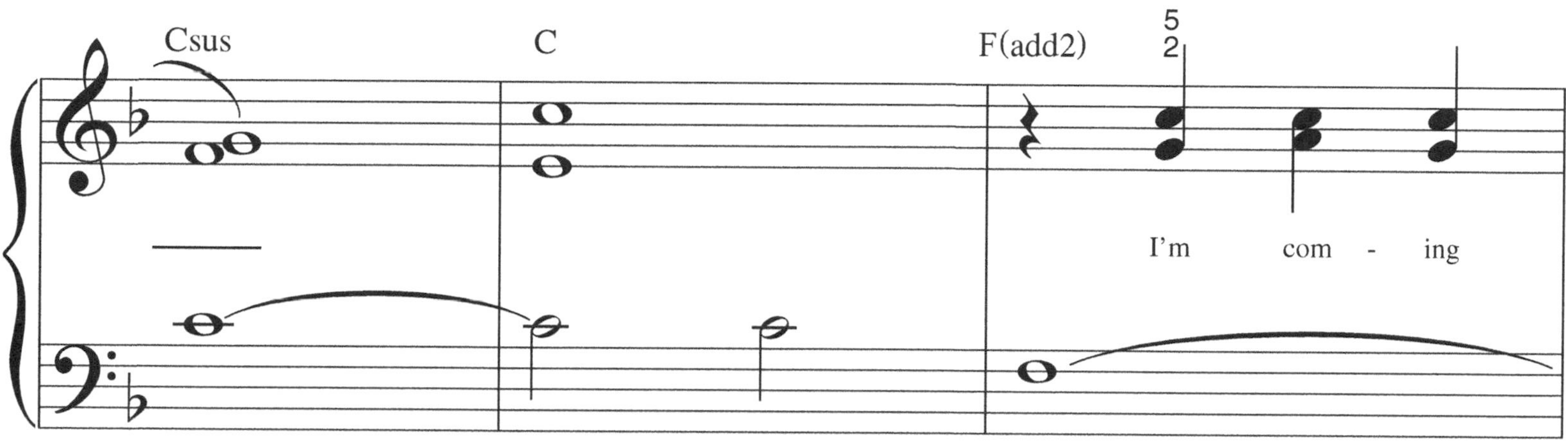
Csus
C
F(add2)
5
2
I'm com - ing

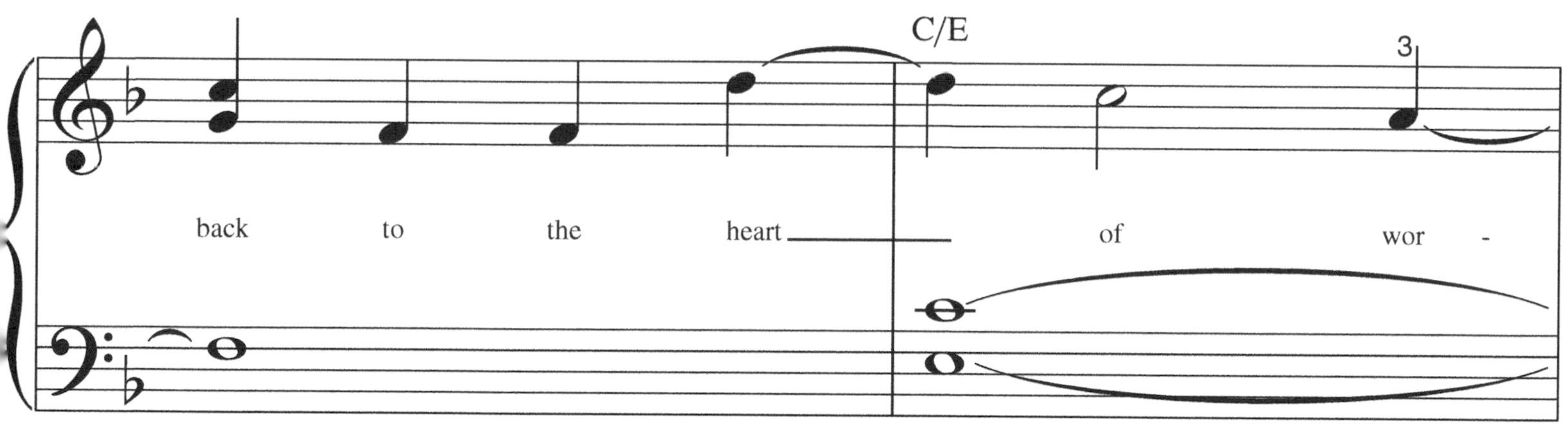
C/E
3
back to the heart of wor -

Gm7
- ship, and it's all a - bout You,

F/A
B♭maj7
Csus
all a - bout You, Je - sus.

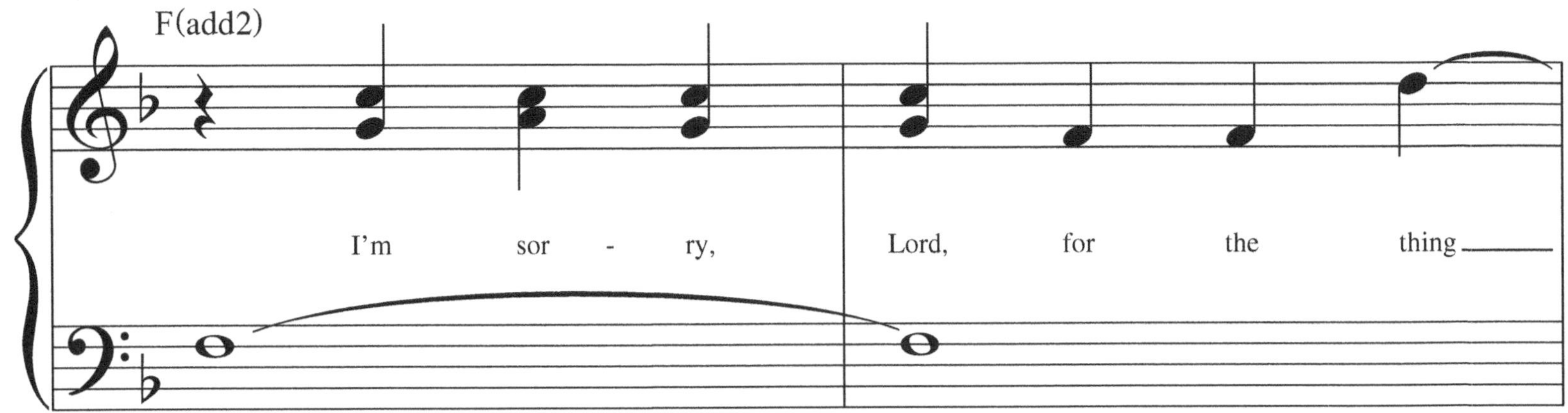
F(add2)
I'm sor - ry, Lord, for the thing

C/E
Gm7
I've made it, when it's all a - bout You,

F/A
B♭maj7
Csus
all a - bout You, Je - sus.

F(add2)
Csus
Gm7
Csus
1.
C
2.
C
F

I COULD SING OF YOUR LOVE FOREVER

Words and Music by
MARTIN SMITH

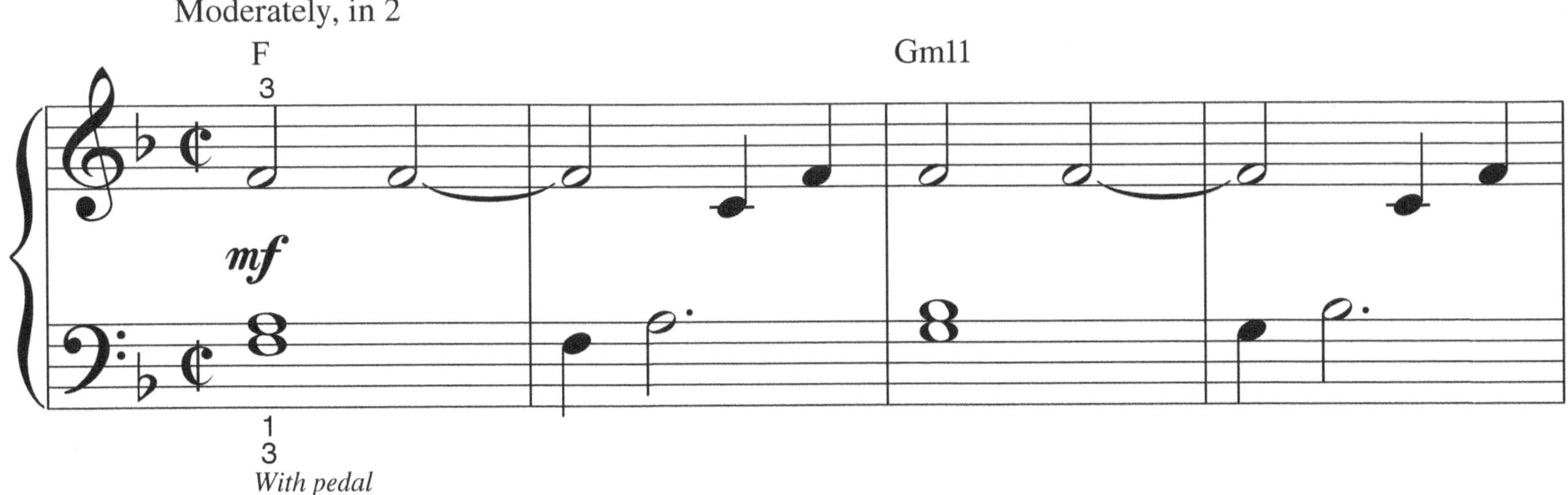

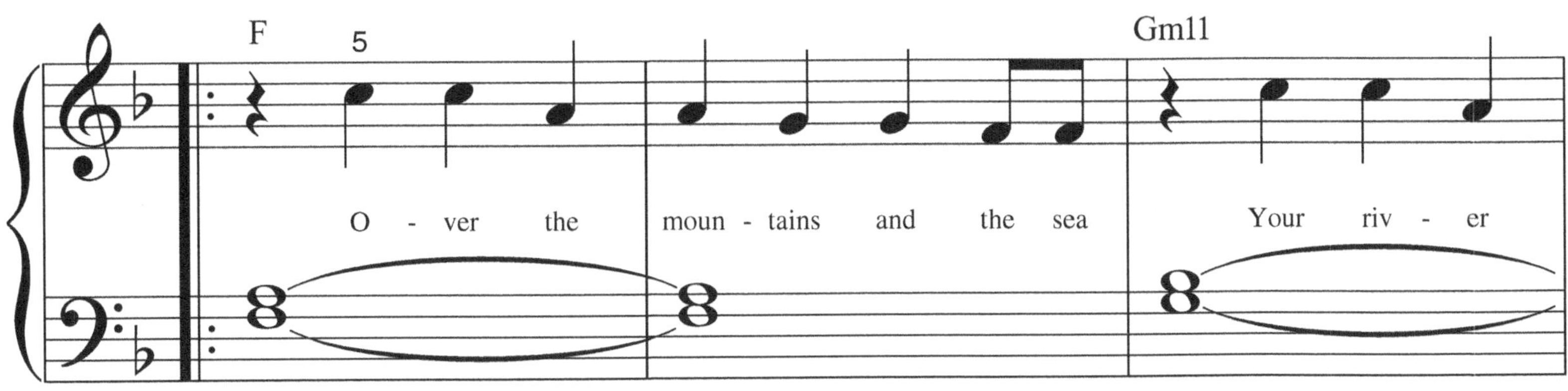

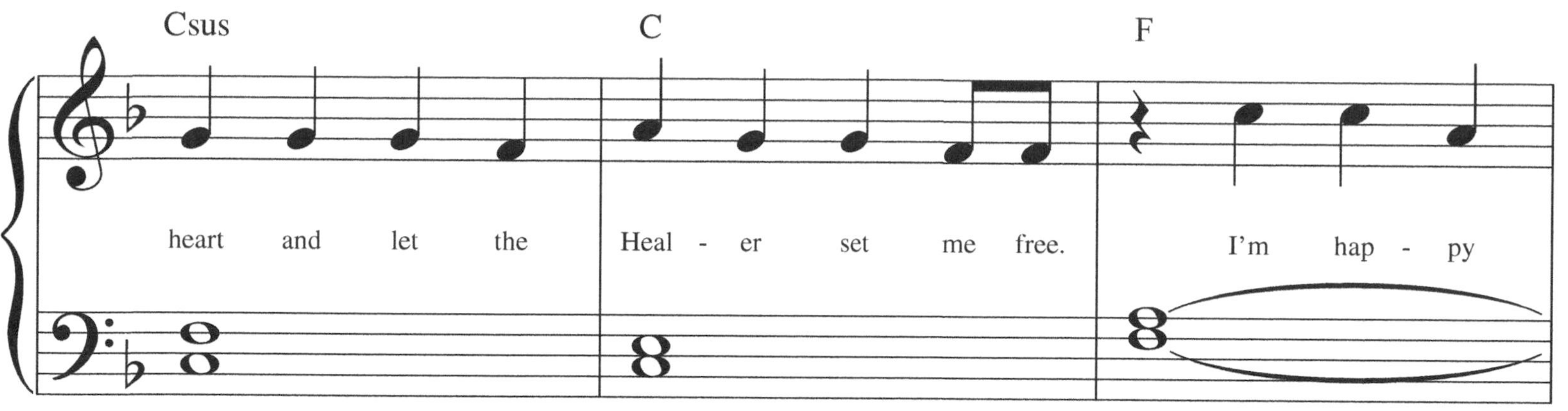
Csus
C
F
heart and let the Heal - er set me free. I'm hap - py

Gm11
to be in the truth and I will dai - ly lift my hands,

B♭sus2
Csus
C
for I will al - ways sing of when Your love came down.

F
Csus
I could sing of Your love for - ev - er,

Dm
B♭sus2
Csus
I could sing of Your love for - ev - er.

F
Csus
I could sing of Your love for - ev - er,

Dm
1.
B♭sus2
Csus
I could sing of Your love for - ev - er.
I could sing of Your love.

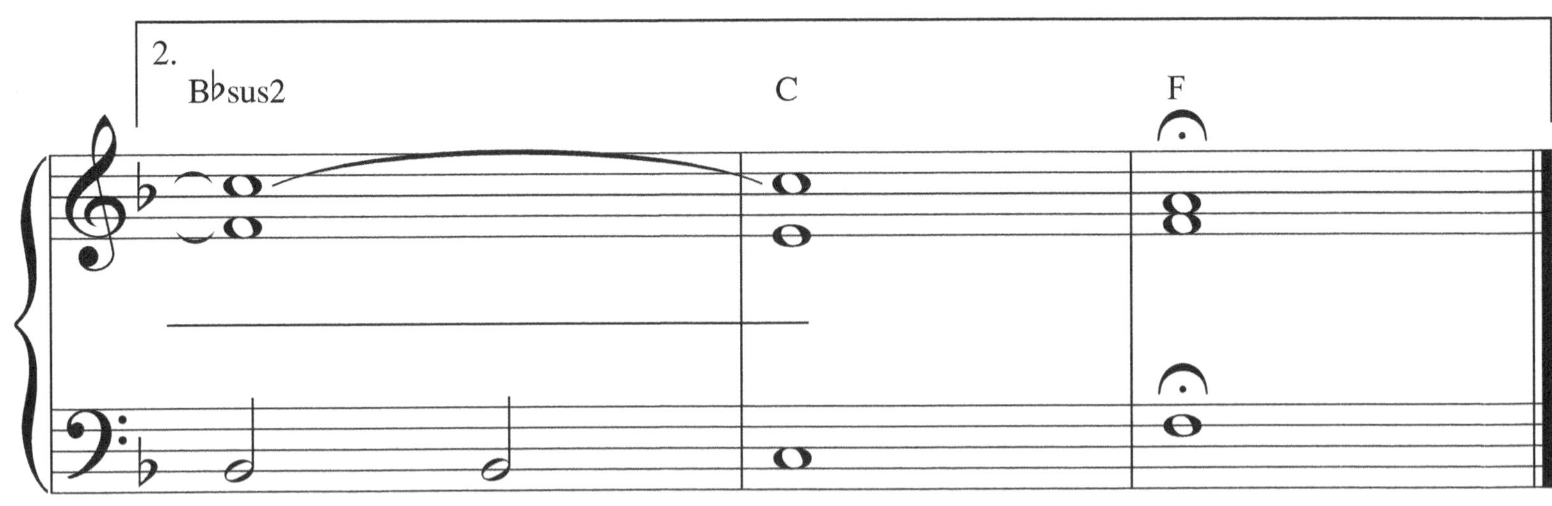
2.
B♭sus2
C
F

OH LORD, YOU'RE BEAUTIFUL

Words and Music by
KEITH GREEN

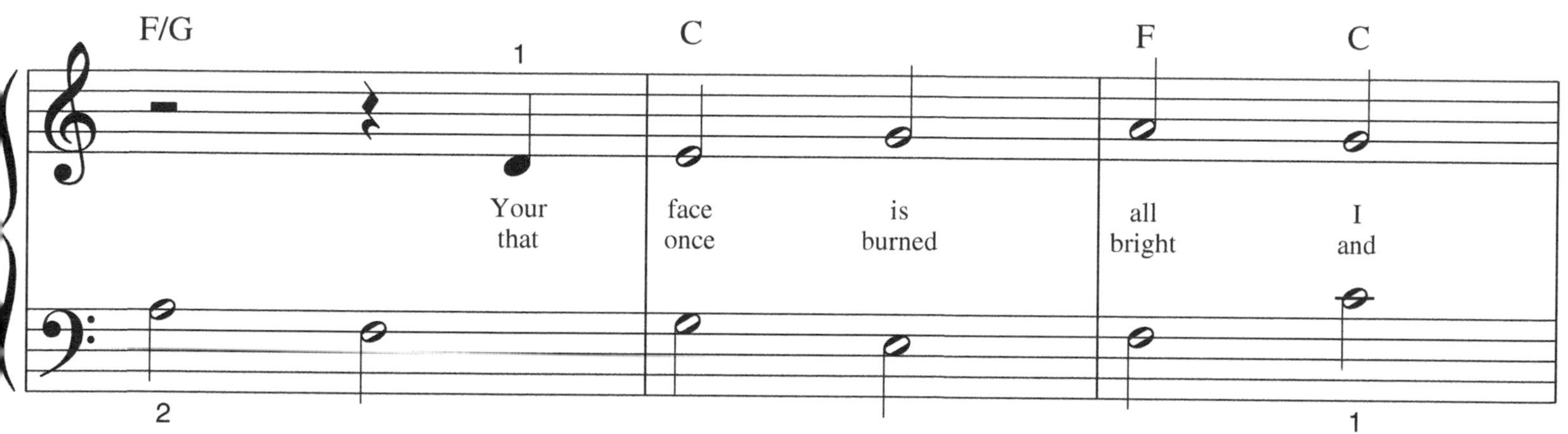

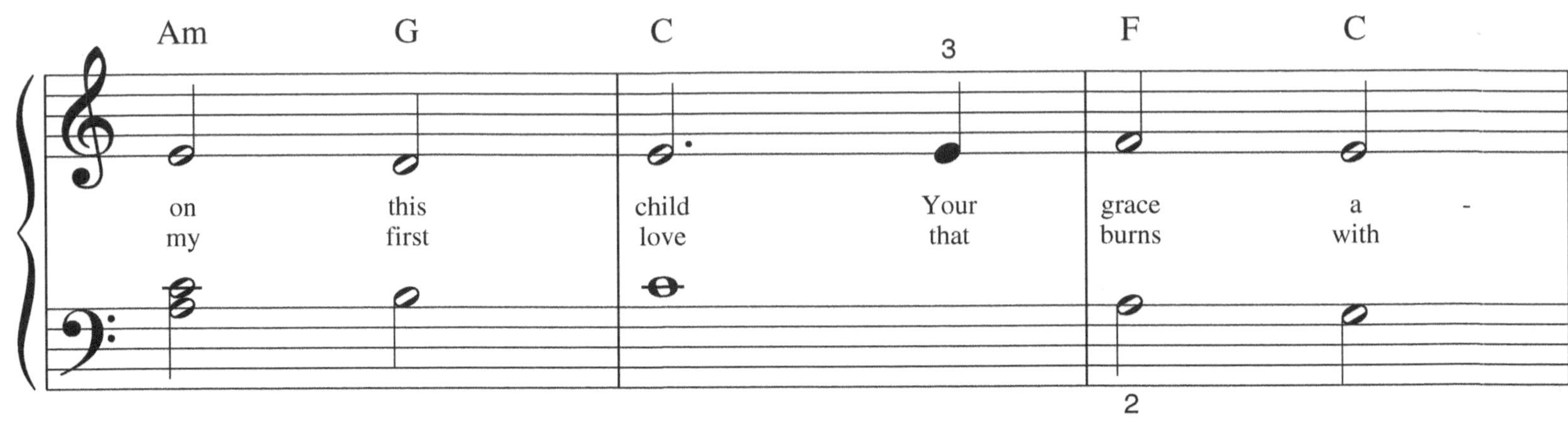
Am G C 3 F C
on this child Your grace a -
my first love that burns with
2

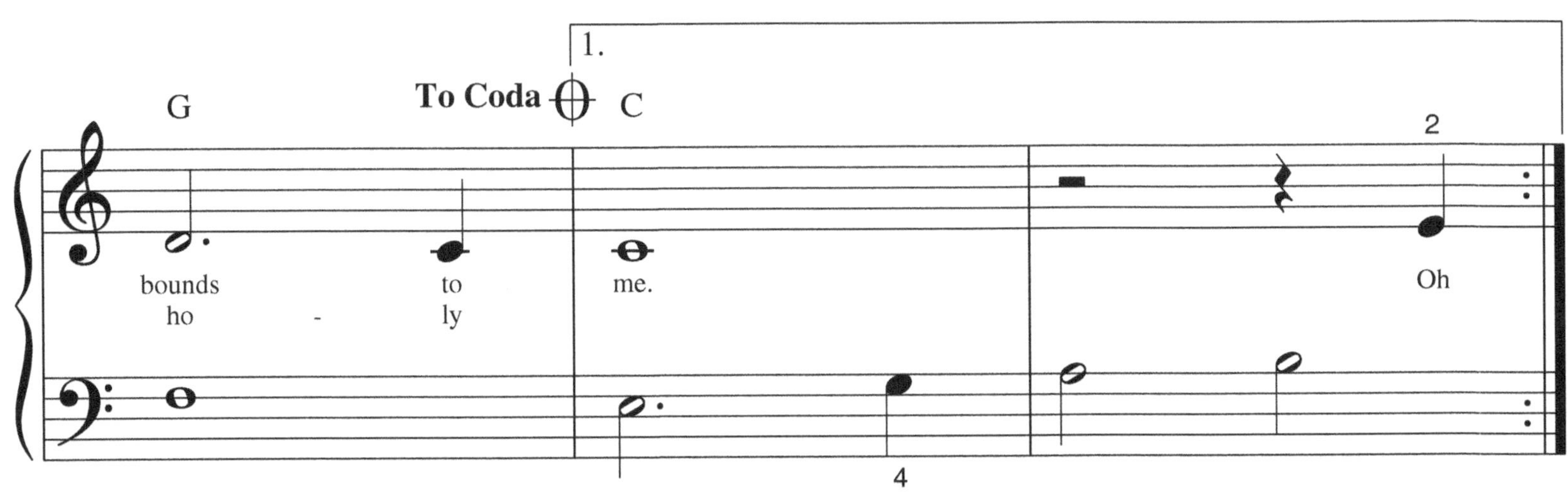
1.
G To Coda C 2
bounds to me. Oh
ho - ly
4

2.
C F C 1 F C/E Dm C
fear. I want to take Your Word and
3 2

G C F D/F♯
2 1
shine it all a - round, but first help me just to live it
4

G
C
F
C/E
2
Lord.
And
when
I'm
do
-
ing
1
2
5

Dm
4
C
G
C
E/G♯
well,
help
me
to
nev
-
er
seek
a
crown,
for
my
re
-
1
3

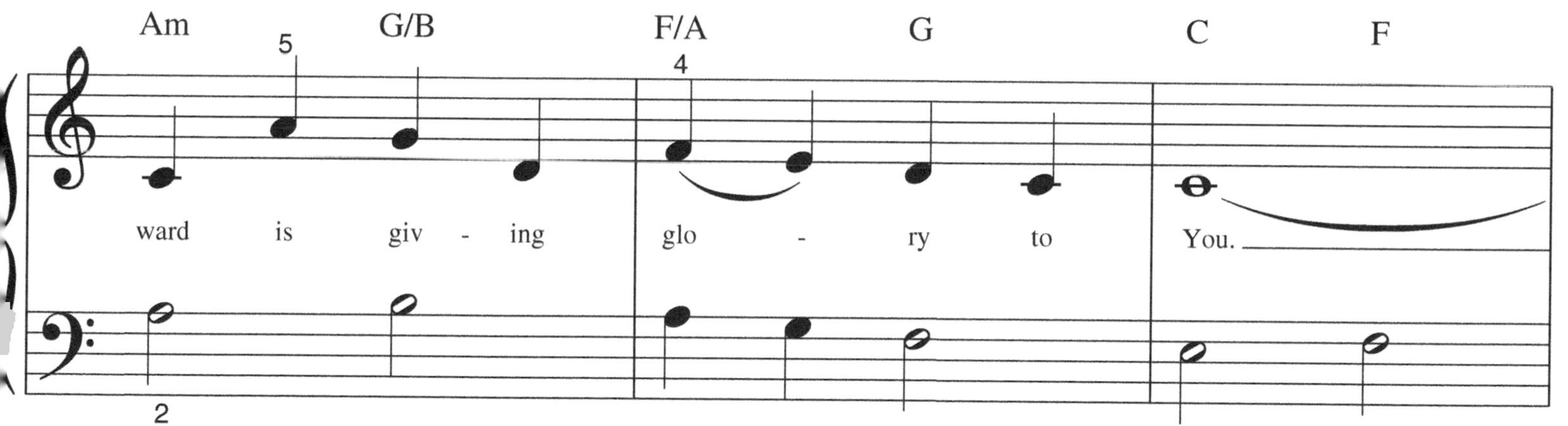
Am
5
G/B
F/A
4
G
C
F
ward
is
giv
-
ing
glo
-
ry
to
You.
2

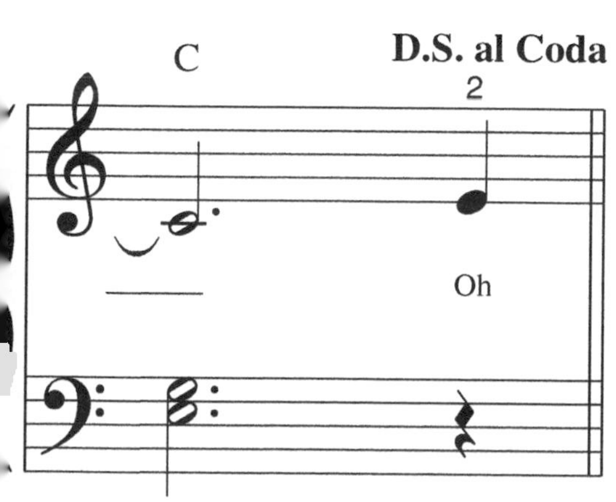
C
D.S. al Coda
2
Oh

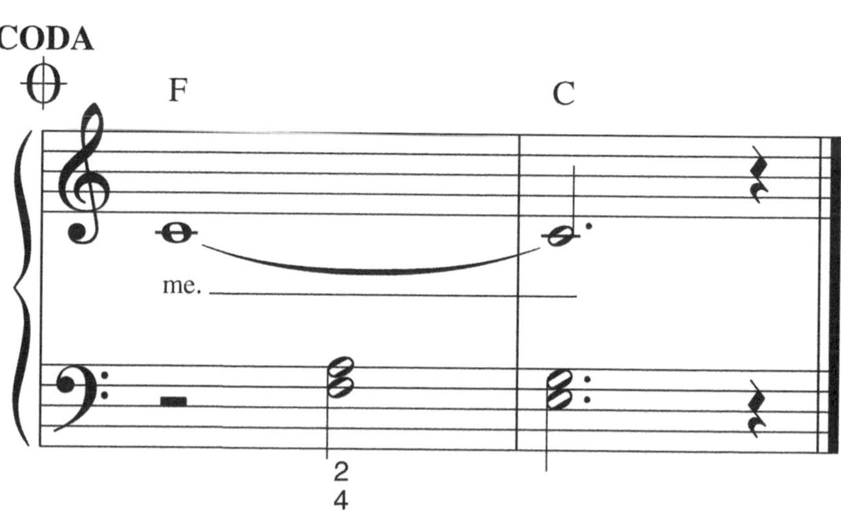
CODA
F
C
me.
2
4

I WANT TO KNOW YOU

Words and Music by
ANDY PARK

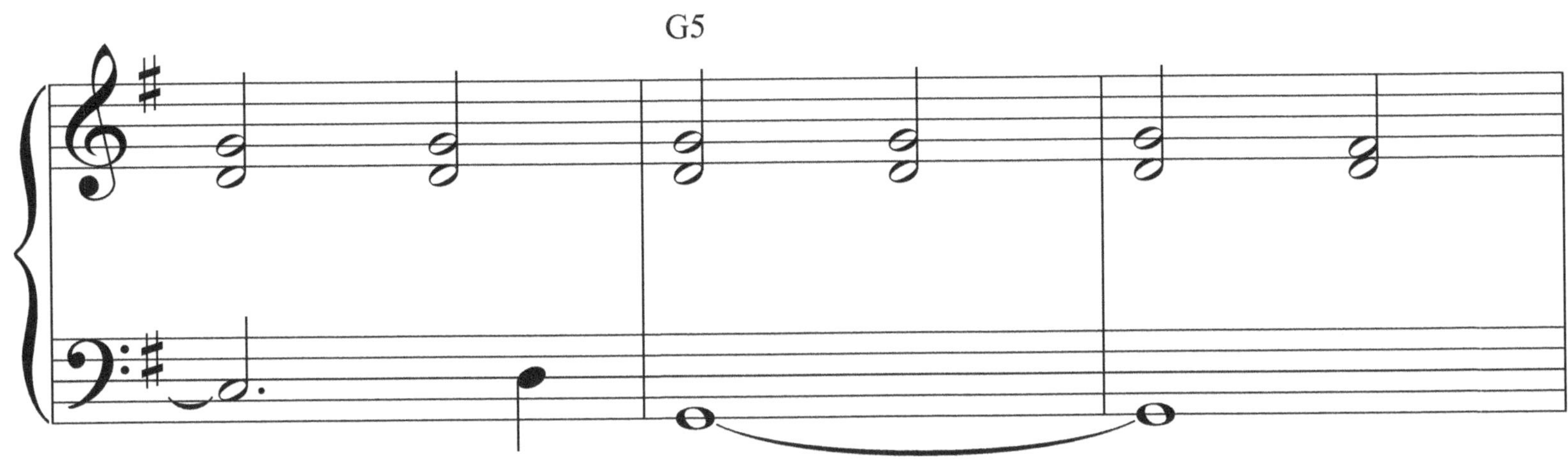

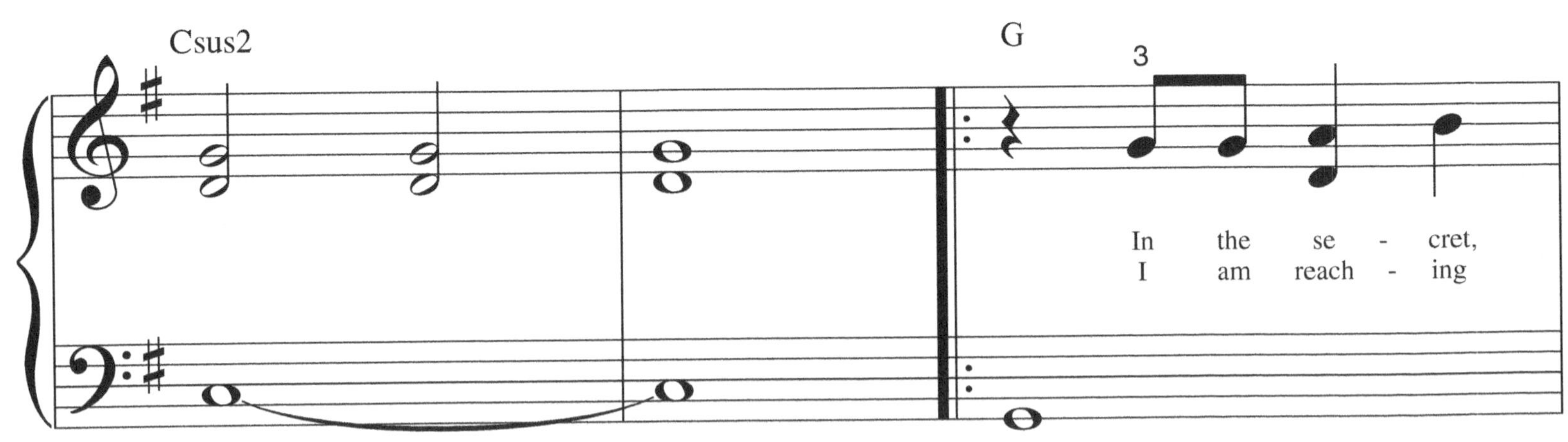

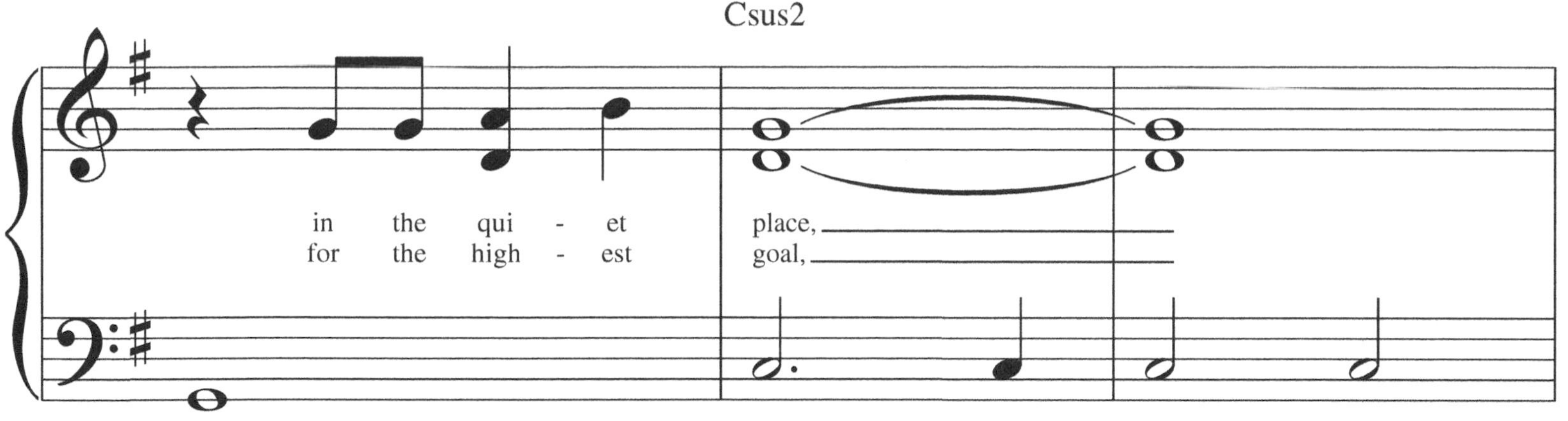
Csus2
in the qui - et
for the high - est
place,
goal,

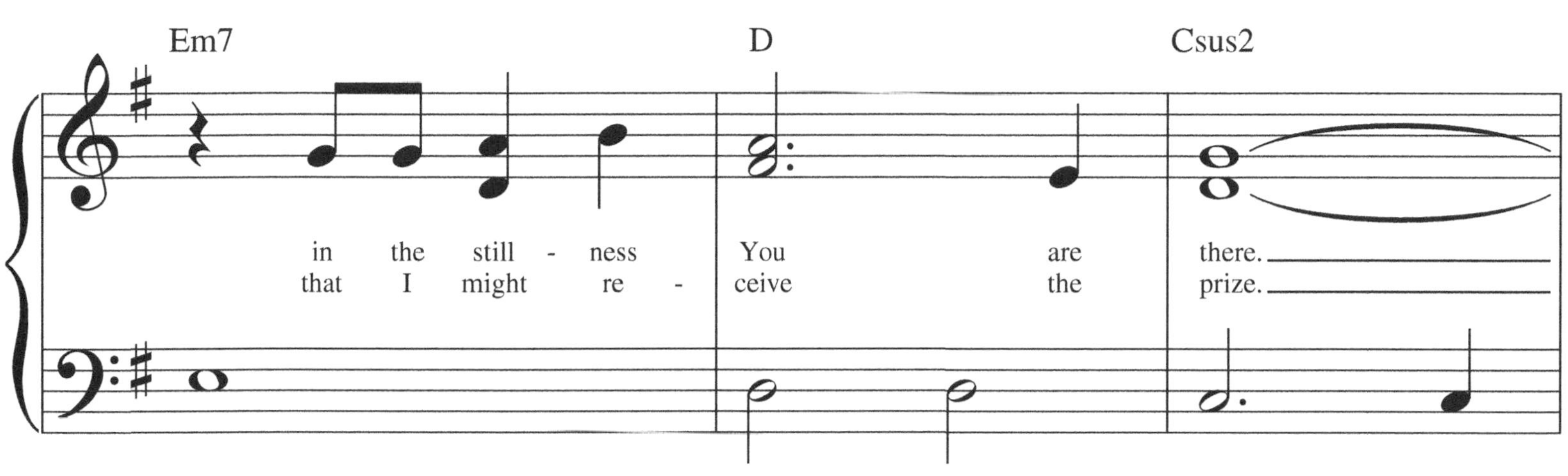
Em7
D
Csus2
in the still - ness
that I might re -
You are
ceive the
there.
prize.

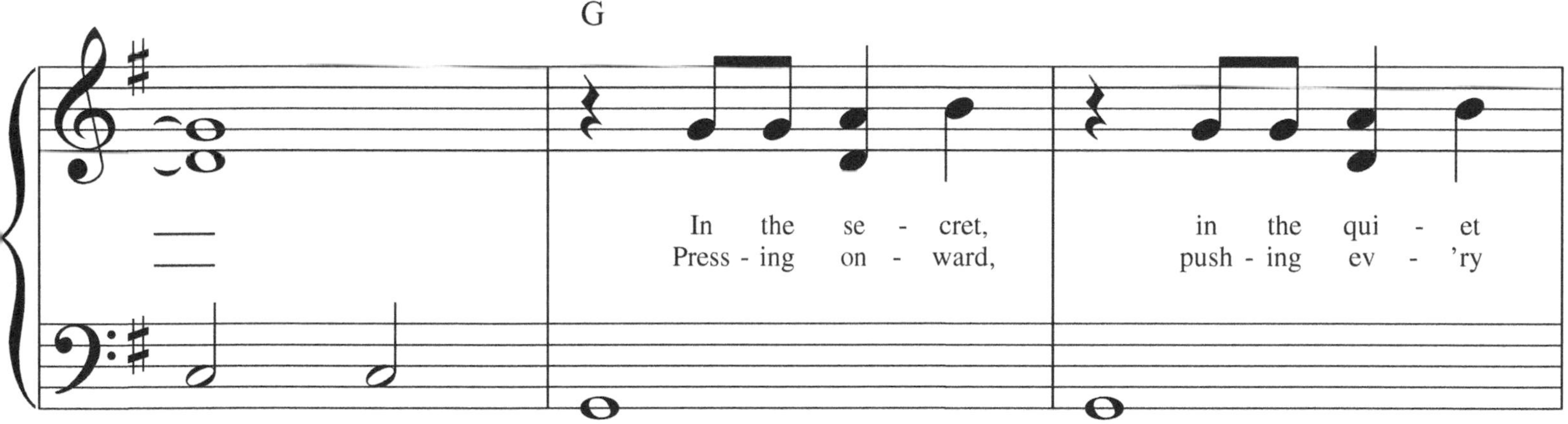
G
In the se - cret,
Press - ing on - ward,
in the qui - et
push - ing ev - 'ry

Csus2
Em7
ho - ur I wait
hin - drance a - side,
on - ly for You,
out of my way,
'cause I want to
'cause I want to

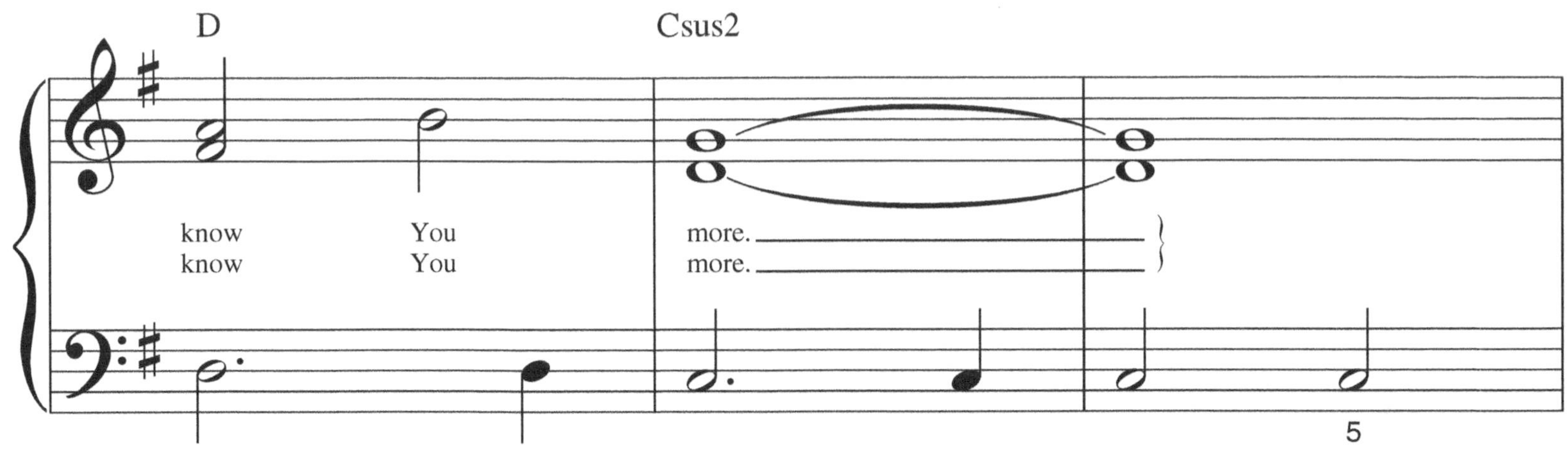
D
Csus2
know You more.
know You more.
5

G
D
Em
1
I want to know You,
I want to

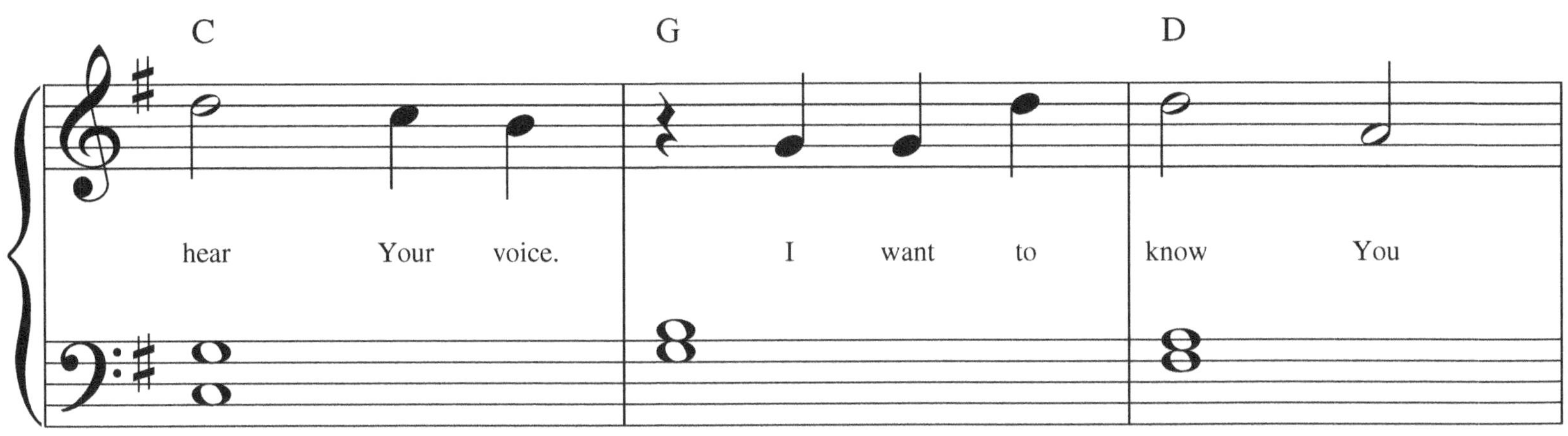
C
G
D
hear Your voice.
I want to know You

Csus2
G
more.
I want to

D
Em
C
touch You, I want to see Your face.

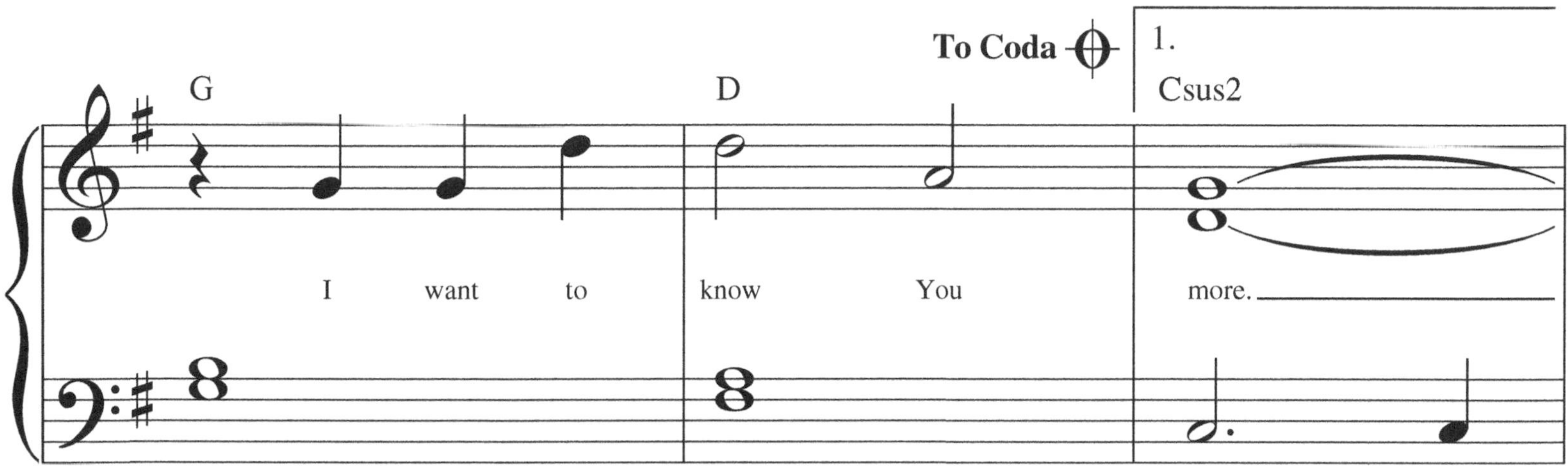
To Coda
1.
G
D
Csus2
I want to know You more.

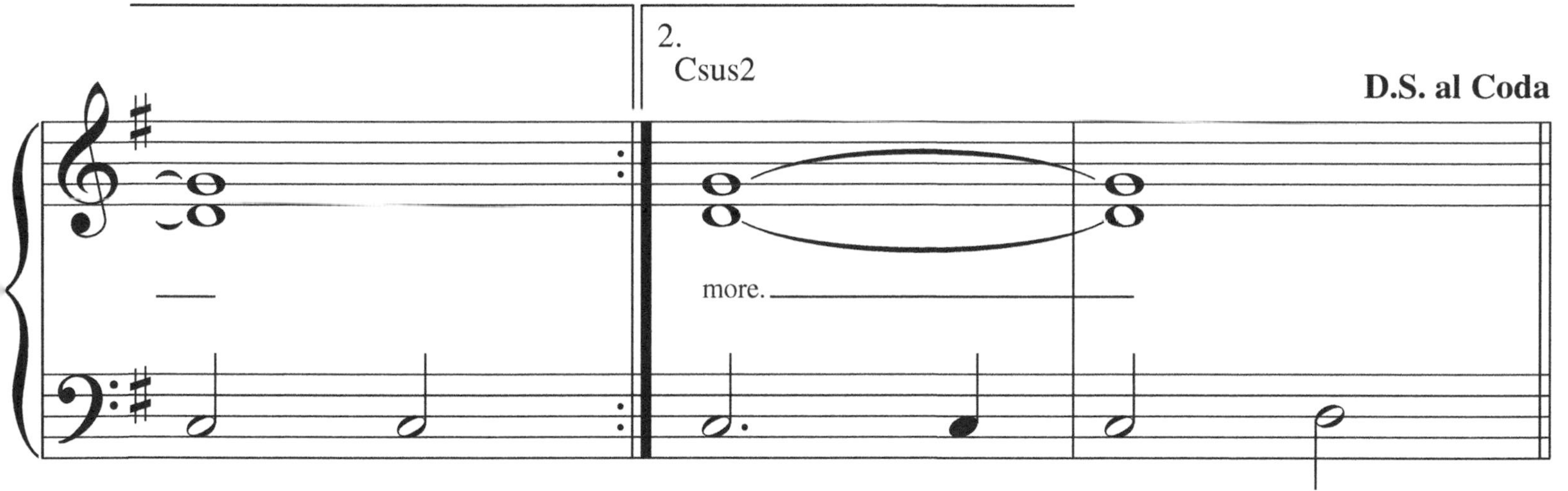
2.
Csus2
D.S. al Coda
more.

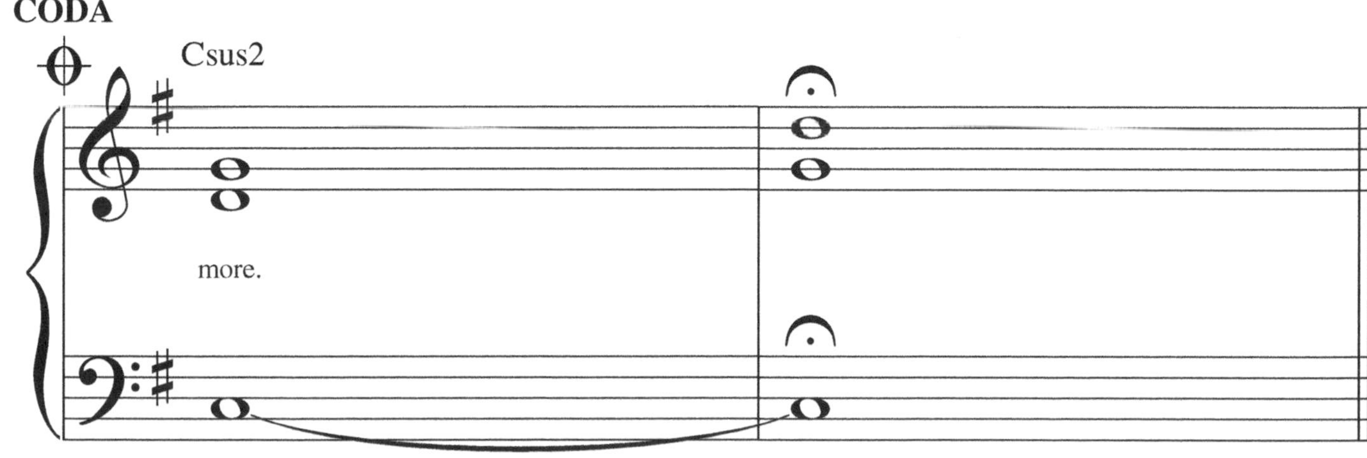
CODA
Csus2
more.

MORE PRECIOUS THAN SILVER

Words and Music by
LYNN DeSHAZO

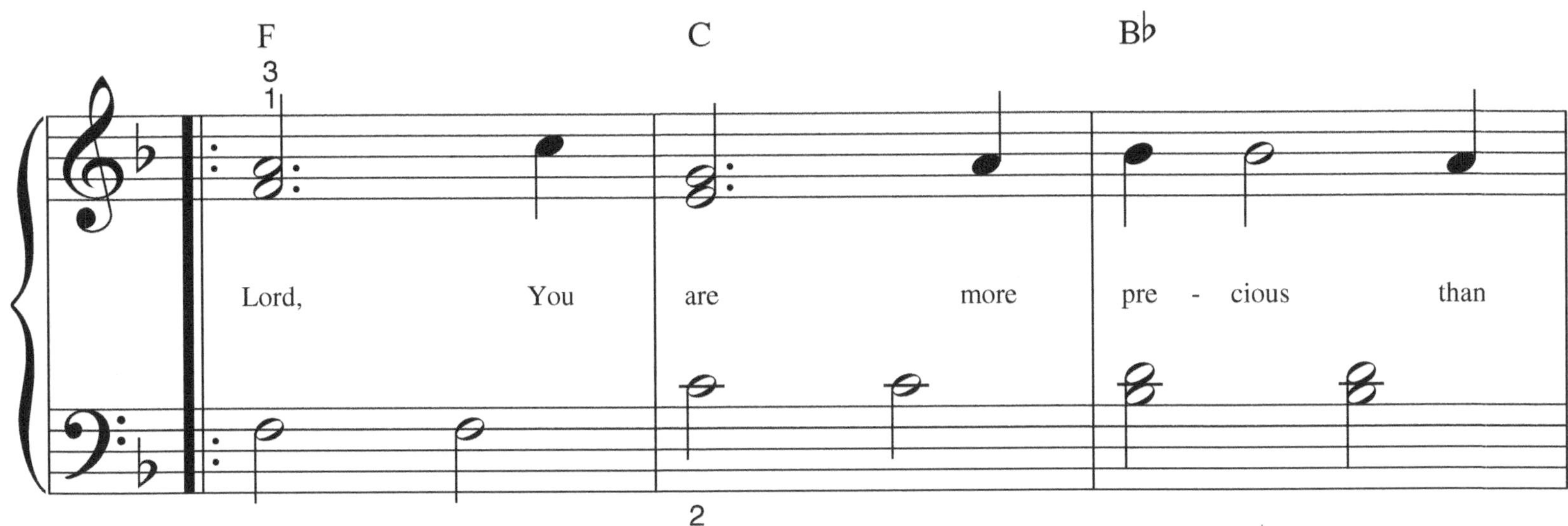

B♭
Csus
C
F
cost - ly than gold.
Lord, You
C
B♭
F/A
are more beau - ti - ful than dia - monds, and
Gm7
F/A
B♭6
Csus
C
1.
Fsus
noth - ing I de - sire com - pares with You.
F
2.
Fsus
F
You.

OPEN THE EYES OF MY HEART

Words and Music by
PAUL BALOCHE

F
F/E
O - pen the eyes of my heart, Lord.
O - pen the eyes of my heart.
I want to see You.
B♭
I want to see You.
Fsus
F
To see You
2
4
C
high and lift - ed up,
Dm
B♭
shin - ing in the light of Your glo - ry.
Csus

C
Dm
B♭
Pour out Your pow - er and
love as we sing
ho - ly, ho - ly,

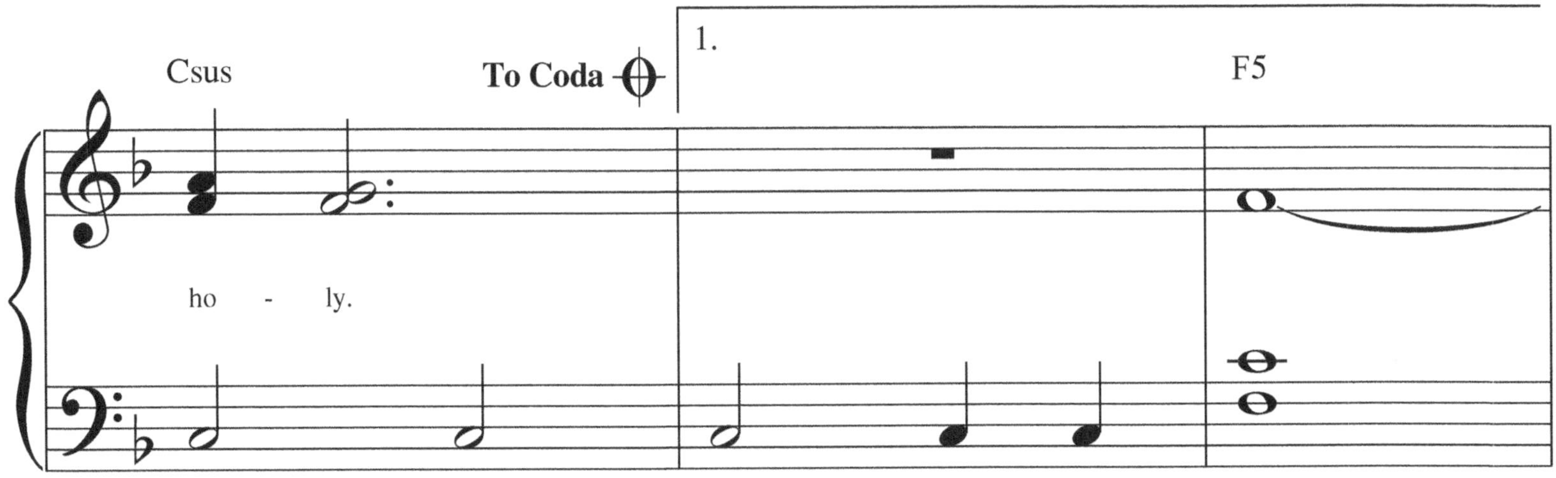
Csus
To Coda
1.
F5
ho - ly.

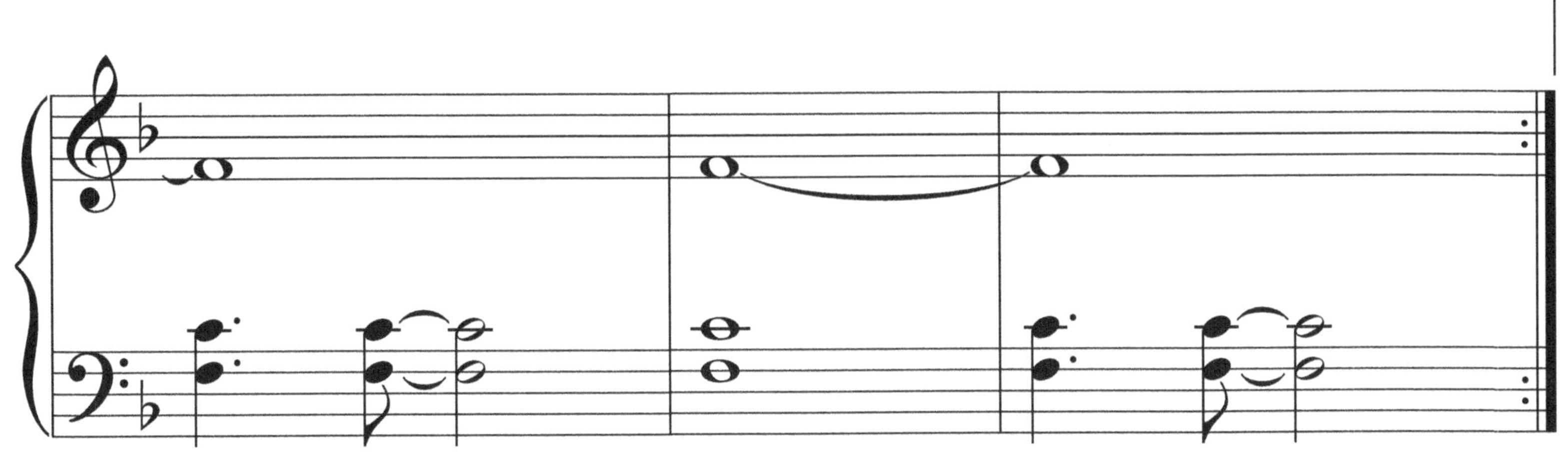

2.
D.S. al Coda
To see You

CODA

F
F/E
Ho - ly, ho - ly, ho - ly.
Ho - ly, ho - ly,
ho - ly.
B♭
Ho - ly, ho - ly,
ho - ly. I want to
F
1.-3.
Fsus
4.
Fsus
F
see You.
I want to see You.
Fsus
F
Fsus
F
I want to see You.
I want to see You.

SHINE, JESUS, SHINE

Words and Music by
GRAHAM KENDRICK

Em
Am
F
G/F
world, shine up - on us,
set us free by the
en - ter Your bright - ness;
search me, try me, con -
glo - ry to glo - ry,
mir - rored here may our
Em
Am
B♭
Gsus
G
truth You now bring us.
sume all my dark - ness.
lives tell Your sto - ry.
Shine on me,
B♭
Gsus
G
C
G/B
shine on me.
Shine, Je - sus,
F/A
Dm
G
shine, fill this land with the Fa - ther's glo - ry.

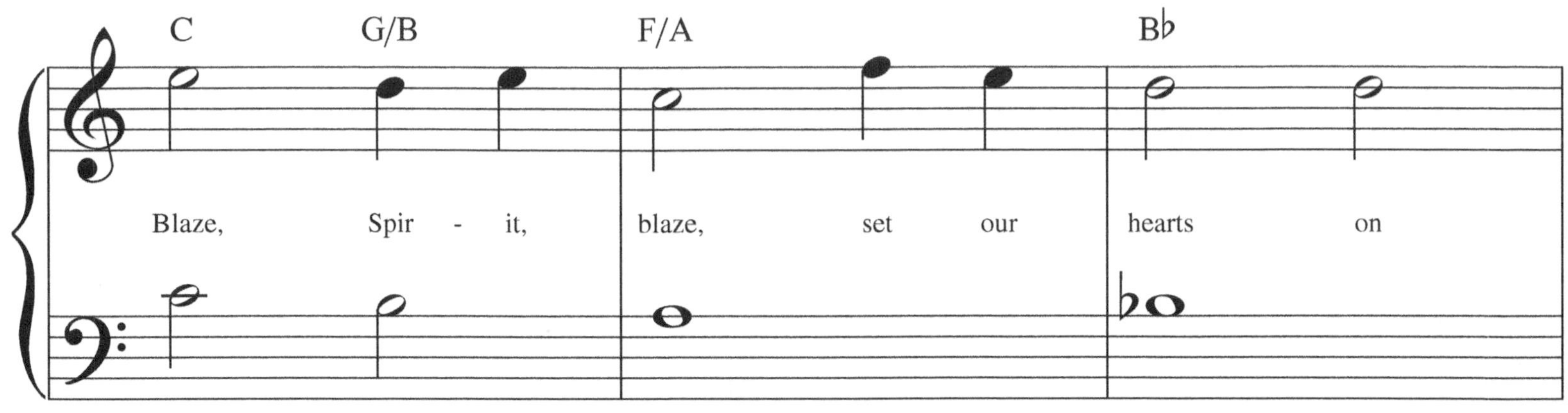
C G/B F/A B♭
Blaze, Spir - it, blaze, set our hearts on

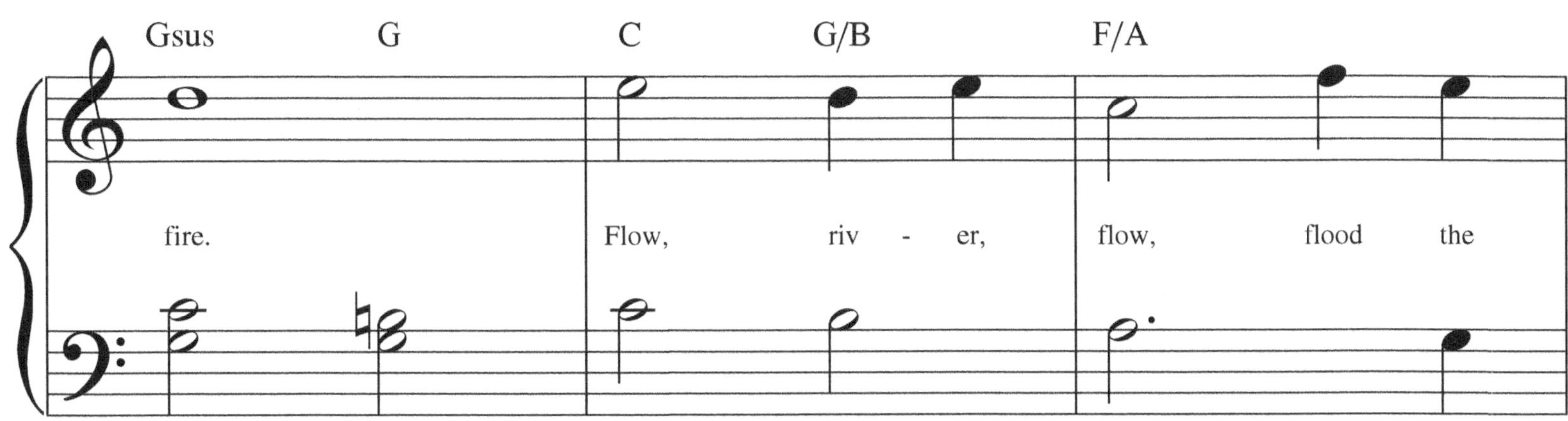
Gsus G C G/B F/A
fire. Flow, riv - er, flow, flood the

Dm G C G/B
na - tions with grace and mer - cy. Send forth Your

F/A Dm G 1., 2. C 3 C
Word, Lord, and let there be light. light.

YOU ARE MY KING
(Amazing Love)

Words and Music by
BILLY JAMES FOOTE

Worshipfully

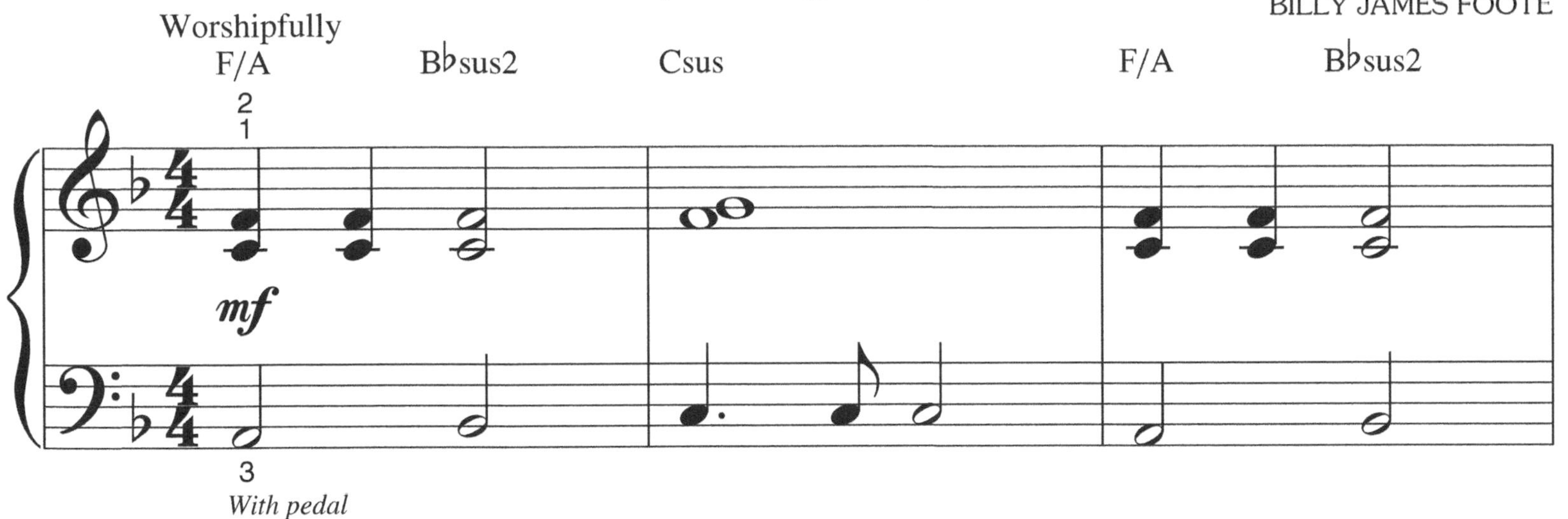

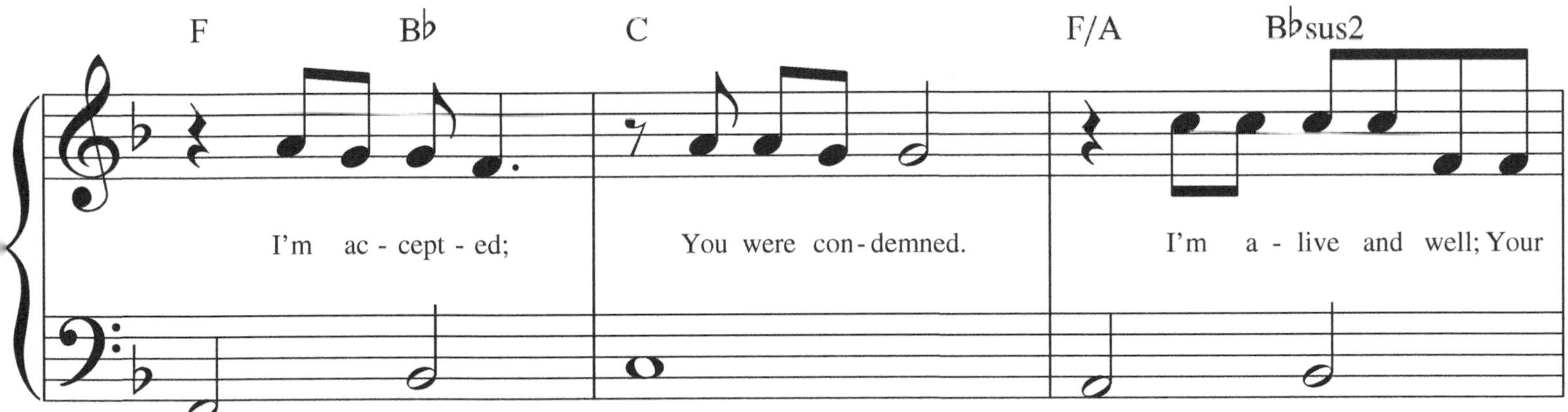

F
F/A
B♭sus2
F/A
A - maz - ing love, how can it be
that You, my King, would die for

C
F
F/A
B♭sus2
me?
A - maz - ing love, I know it's true;

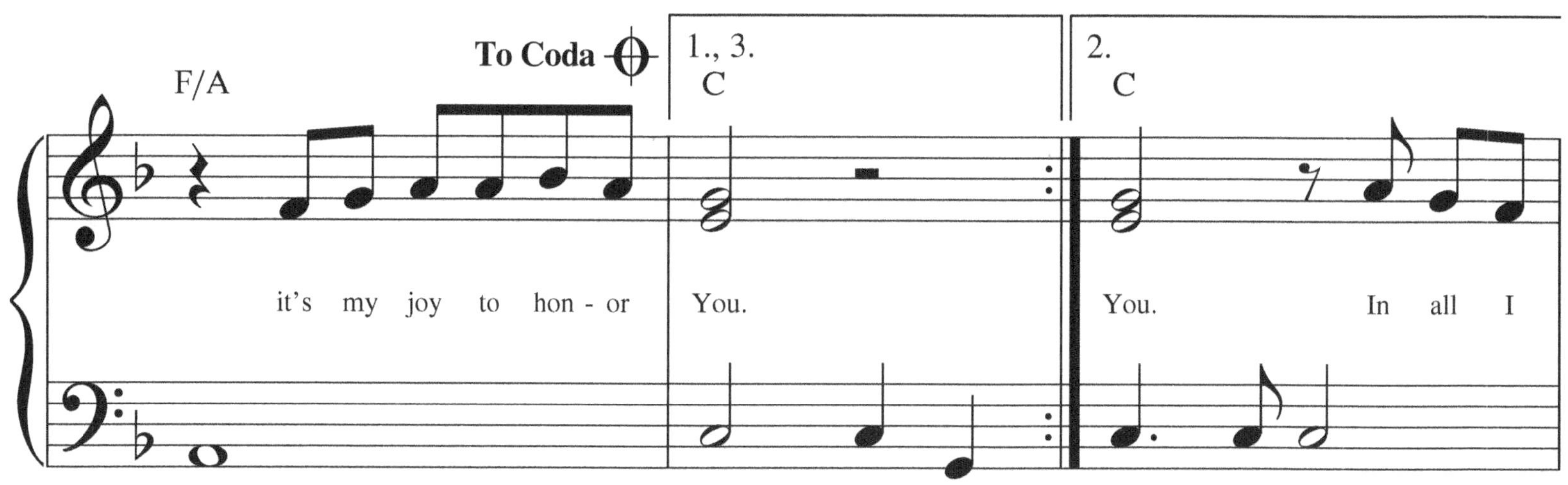
F/A
To Coda
1., 3.
C
2.
C
it's my joy to hon - or You.
You. In all I

B♭
C
F
do, I hon - or You.
You are my

King.
You are my King. Je - sus, You are my

D.S. al Coda
(with repeat)
King. Je - sus, You are my King.

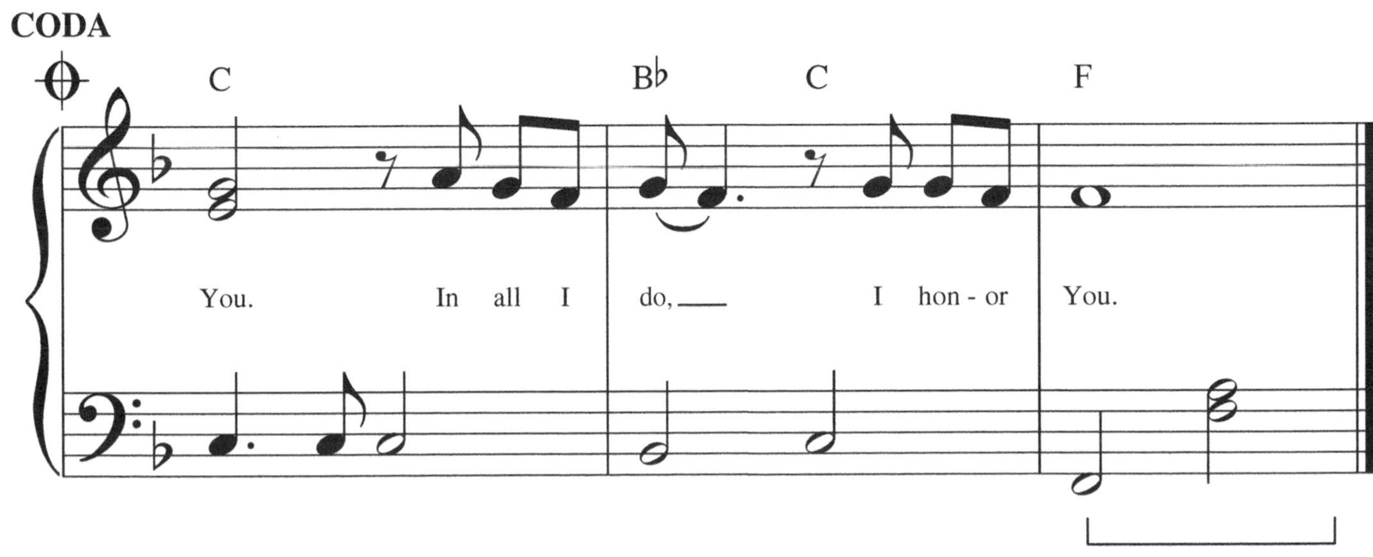
CODA
C
B♭
C
F
You. In all I do, I hon - or You.

SHOUT TO THE LORD

Words and Music by
DARLENE ZSCHECH

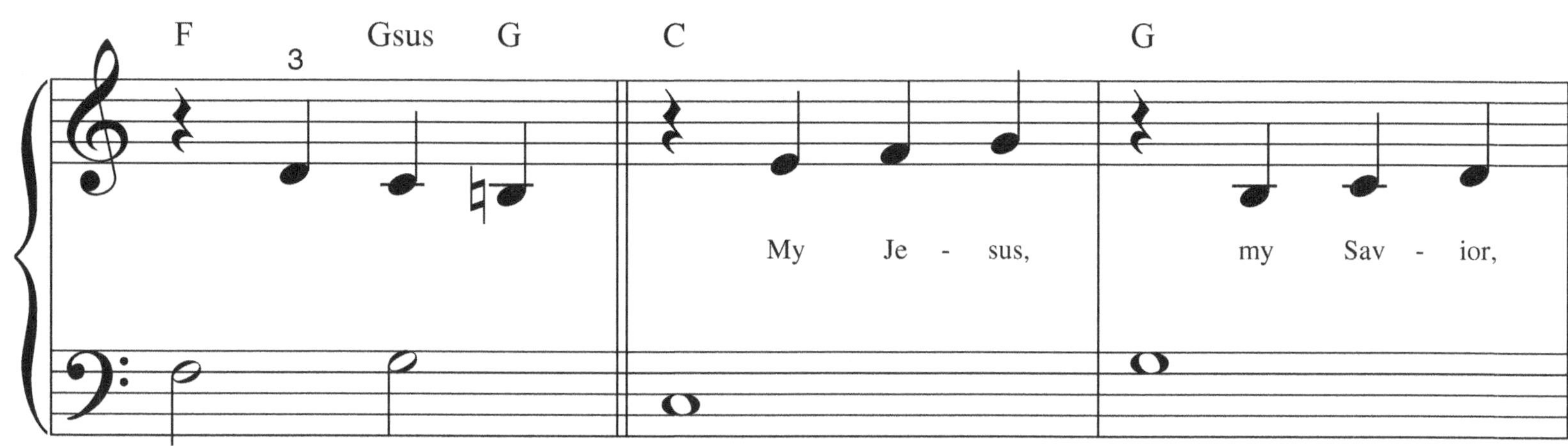

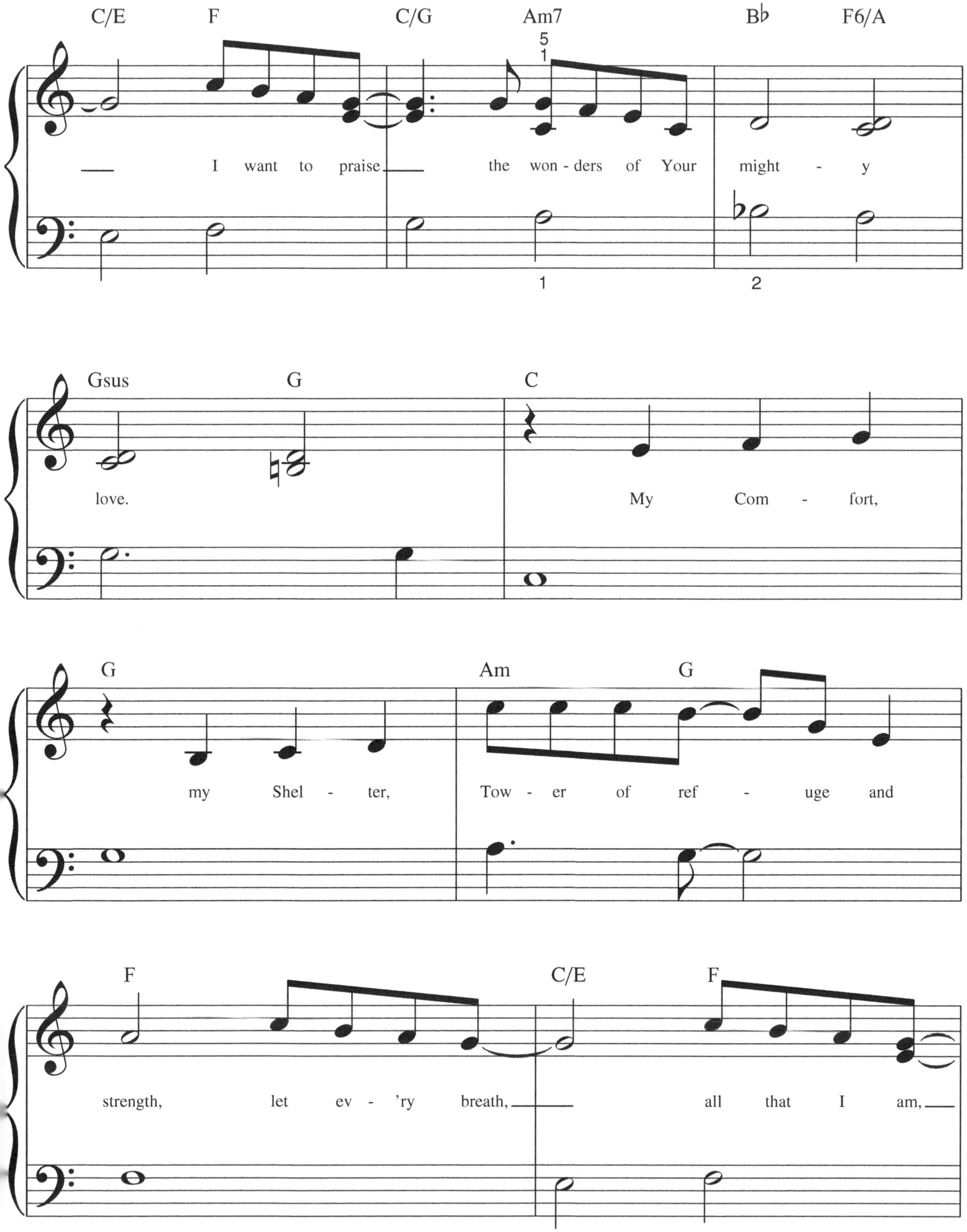

C/E F C/G Am7 B♭ F6/A

5 1

I want to praise the won - ders of Your might - y

1 2

Gsus G C

love. My Com - fort,

G Am G

my Shel - ter, Tow - er of ref - uge and

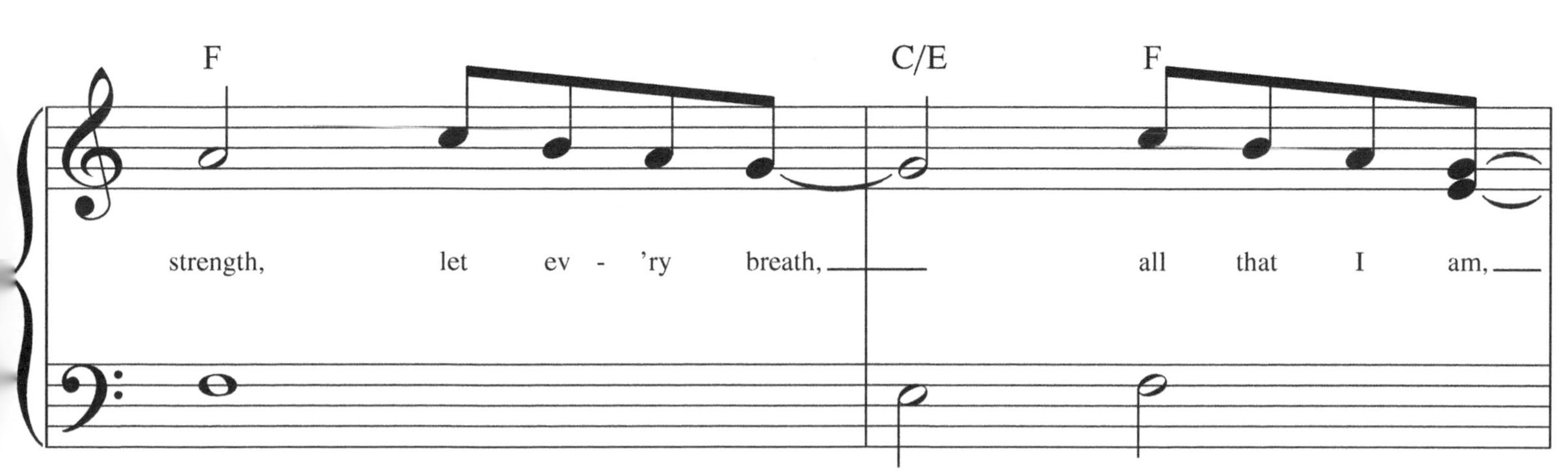

C/G Am Bb F6/A Gsus G
never cease to wor - ship You.
C Am F G
Shout to the Lord, all the earth, let us sing;
C Am F G
pow - er and maj - es - ty, praise to the King!
Am F
Moun - tains bow down and the seas will roar at the

G
Am
G/B
sound of Your name.

C
Am
F
G
3
I sing for joy at the work of Your hands, for -

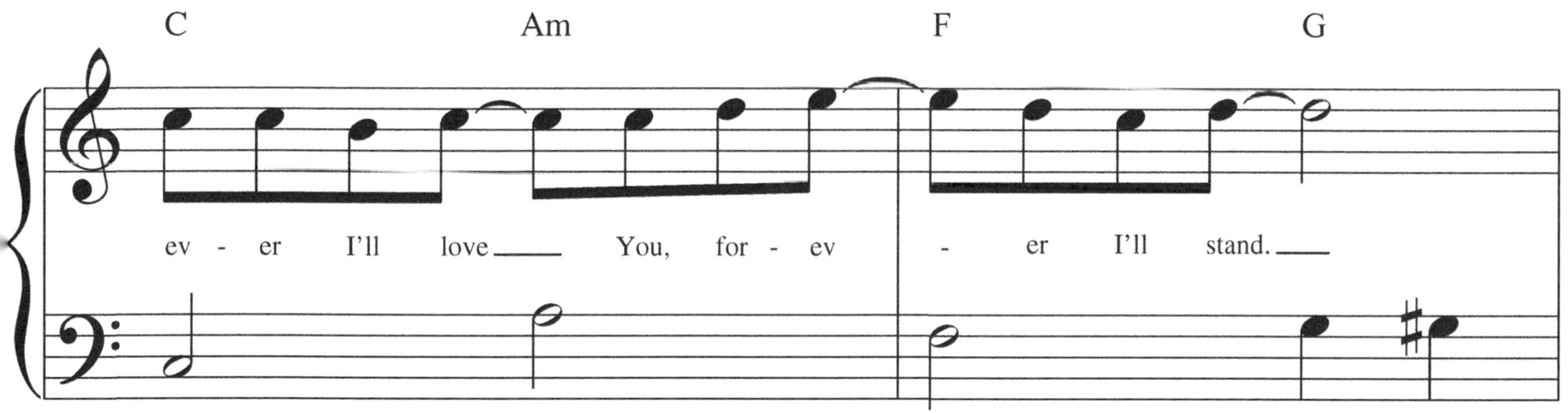
C
Am
F
G
ev - er I'll love You, for - ev - er I'll stand.

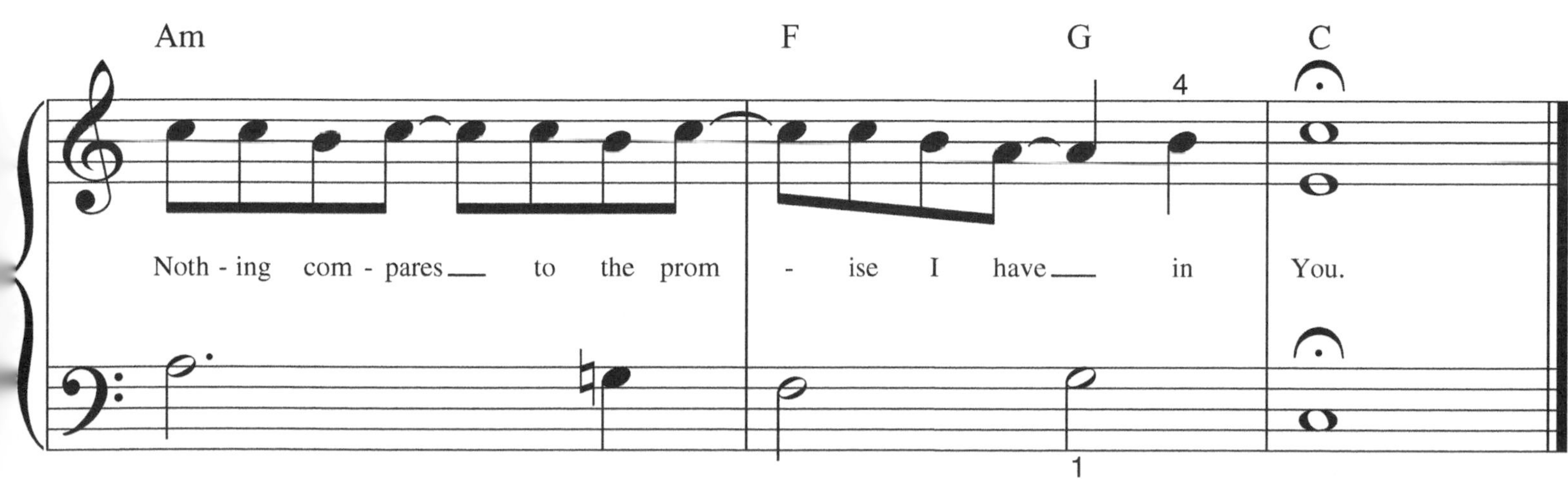
Am
F
G
C
4
Noth - ing com - pares to the prom - ise I have in You.
1

WORTHY IS THE LAMB

Words and Music by
DARLENE ZSCHECH

G/B C F C/E C
grace. Thank you for this love, Lord. Thank you for the
1
F G/B C Am7
nail - pierced hands. Washed me in Your cleans - ing flow, now
G F Dm7 C/E Gsus G
4
3
all I know, Your for - give - ness and em - brace.
C G/B Dm7 C/E
Wor - thy is the Lamb seat - ed on the
4

F
G
G/F
C/E
F
3
1
throne.
Crown You now with
man - y crowns, You
2
1

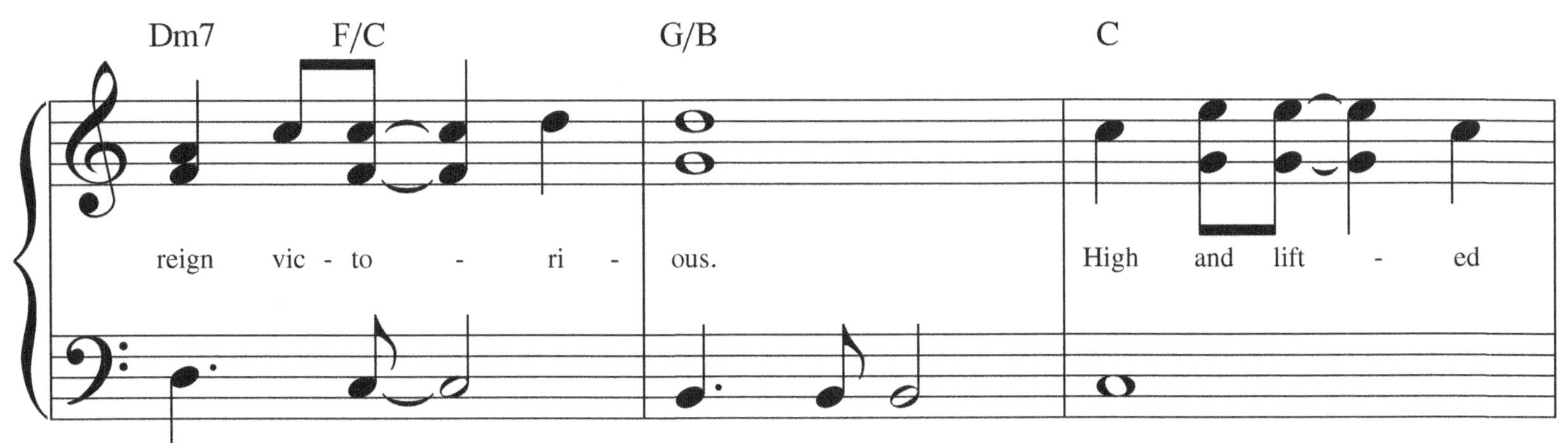
Dm7
F/C
G/B
C
reign vic - to - ri - ous.
High and lift - ed

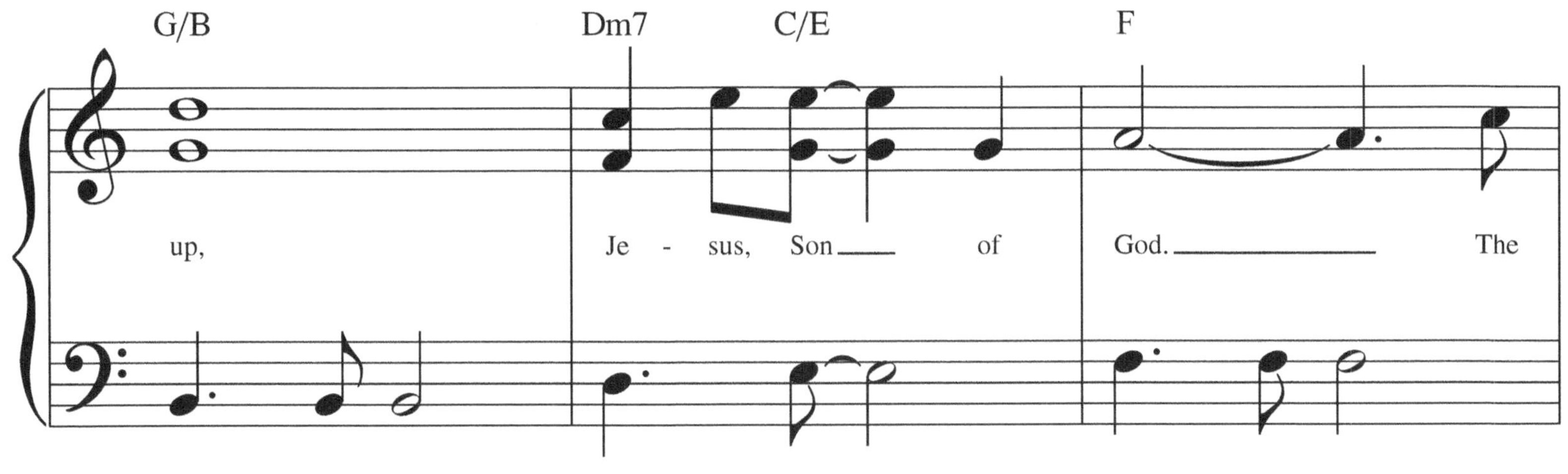
G/B
Dm7
C/E
F
up,
Je - sus, Son of
God. The

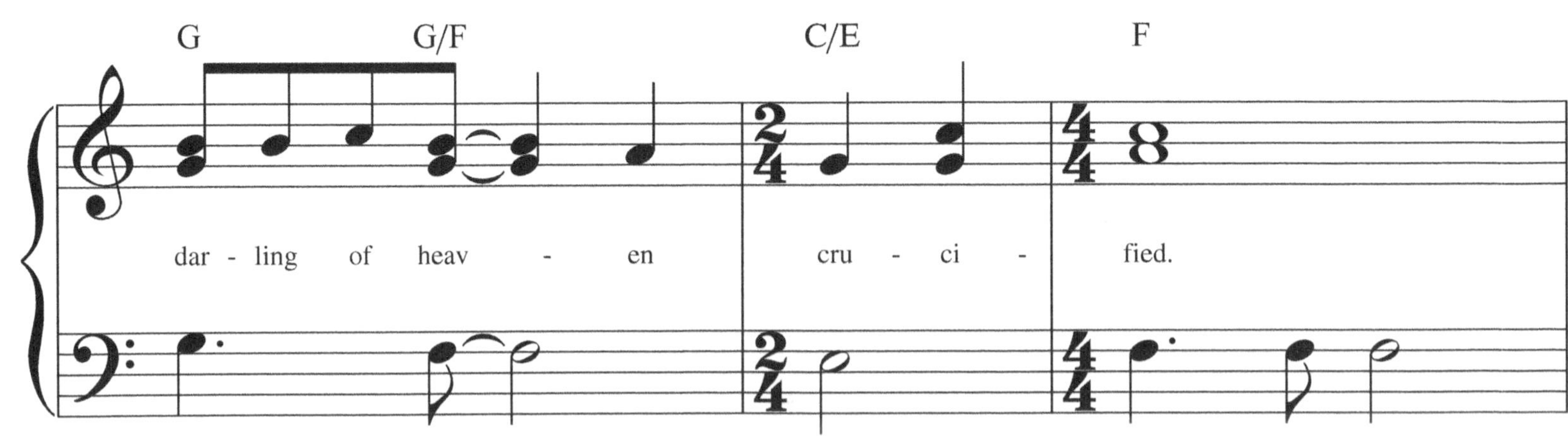
G
G/F
C/E
F
dar - ling of heav - en
cru - ci - fied.

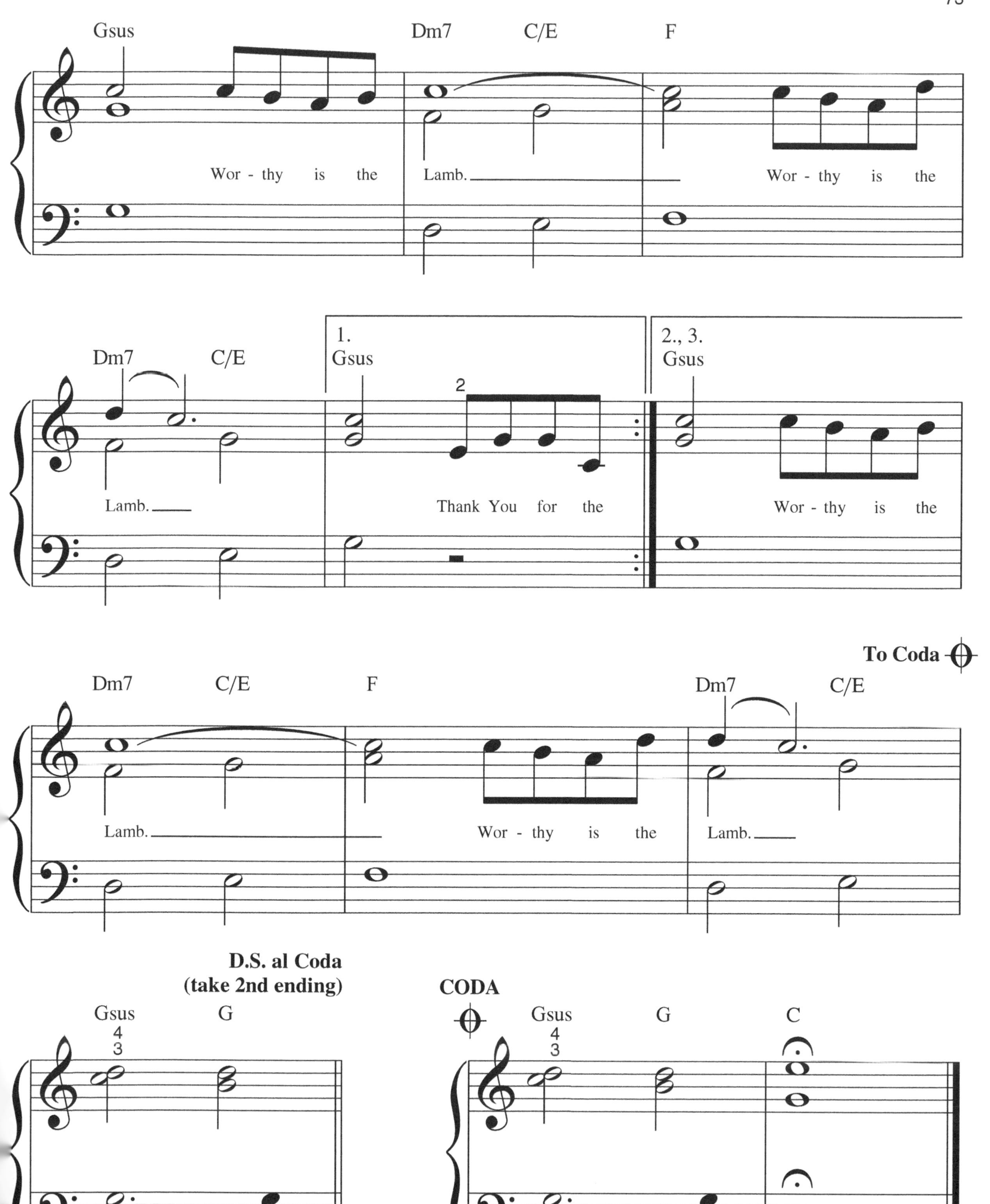
Gsus
Dm7
C/E
F
Wor - thy is the
Lamb.
Wor - thy is the
Dm7
C/E
1.
Gsus
2., 3.
Gsus
Lamb.
Thank You for the
Wor - thy is the
To Coda
Dm7
C/E
F
Dm7
C/E
Lamb.
Wor - thy is the
Lamb.
D.S. al Coda
(take 2nd ending)
Gsus
G
CODA
Gsus
G
C

STEP BY STEP

Words and Music by
DAVID STRASSER "BEAKER"

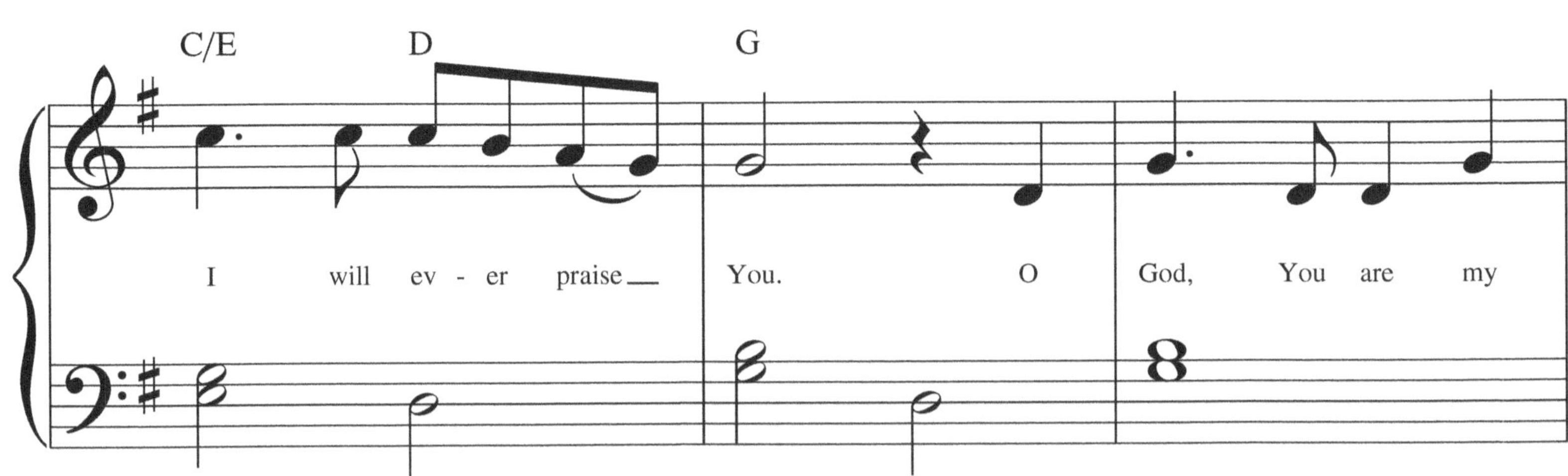

D/F#
C/E
D
G
God, and I will ev - er praise You. I will
Em
D
C
seek You in the morn - ing and I will learn to walk in Your
C/D
G
D/F#
ways. And step by step You'll lead me, and I will
C/E
D
1.
G
C/E
D/F#
fol - low You all of my days. O

2.
G
Em
Dsus
D
2
days. And I will
fol - low You all of my
days, and I will

C
C/D
G
5
fol - low You all of my
days. And
step by step You'll

D/F♯
C/E
D
G
5
lead me, and I will
fol - low You all of my
days.
rit.

THE BIG BOOK OF HYMNS
The BIG BOOK of HYMNS

THE BEST GOSPEL SONGS EVER
GOSPEL SONGS

THE PHILLIP KEVEREN SERIES PIANO SOLO
THE HYMN COLLECTION

HAL•LEONARD®
CORPORATION

Big Fun with Big-Note Piano Books!

These songbooks feature exciting easy arrangements for beginning piano students.

Best of Adele
Now even beginners can play their favorite Adele tunes! This book features big-note arrangements of 10 top songs: Chasing Pavements • Daydreamer • Hometown Glory • Lovesong • Make You Feel My Love • One and Only • Rolling in the Deep • Set Fire to the Rain • Someone like You • Turning Tables.
00308601 .... $14.99

Beatles' Best
27 classics for beginners to enjoy, including: Can't Buy Me Love • Eleanor Rigby • Hey Jude • Michelle • Here, There and Everywhere • When I'm Sixty-Four • Yesterday • and more.
00222561 .... $14.99

The Best Songs Ever
70 favorites, featuring: Body and Soul • Crazy • Edelweiss • Fly Me to the Moon • Georgia on My Mind • Imagine • The Lady Is a Tramp • Memory • A String of Pearls • Tears in Heaven • Unforgettable • You Are So Beautiful • and more.
00310425 .... $19.95

Children's Favorite Movie Songs
arranged by Phillip Keveren
16 favorites from films, including: The Bare Necessities • Beauty and the Beast • Can You Feel the Love Tonight • Do-Re-Mi • The Rainbow Connection • Tomorrow • Zip-A-Dee-Doo-Dah • and more.
00310838 .... $12.99

Classical Music's Greatest Hits
24 beloved classical pieces, including: Air on the G String • Ave Maria • By the Beautiful Blue Danube • Canon in D • Eine Kleine Nachtmusik • Für Elise • Ode to Joy • Romeo and Juliet • Waltz of the Flowers • more.
00310475 .... $12.99

Disney Big-Note Collection
Over 40 Disney favorites, including: Circle of Life • Colors of the Wind • Hakuna Matata • It's a Small World • Under the Sea • A Whole New World • Winnie the Pooh • Zip-A-Dee-Doo-Dah • and more.
00316056 .... $19.99

Essential Classical
22 simplified piano pieces from top composers, including: Ave Maria (Schubert) • Blue Danube Waltz (Strauss) • Für Elise (Beethoven) • Jesu, Joy of Man's Desiring (Bach) • Morning (Grieg) • Pomp and Circumstance (Elgar) • and many more.
00311205 .... $10.99

Favorite Children's Songs
arranged by Bill Boyd
29 easy arrangements of songs to play and sing with children: Peter Cottontail • I Whistle a Happy Tune • It's a Small World • On the Good Ship Lollipop • The Rainbow Connection • and more!
00240251 .... $12.99

Frozen
9 songs from this hit Disney film, plus full-color illustrations from the movie. Songs include the standout single "Let It Go", plus: Do You Want to Build a Snowman? • For the First Time in Forever • Reindeer(s) Are Better Than People • and more.
00126105 .... $12.99

Happy Birthday to You and Other Great Songs for Big-Note Piano
16 essential favorites, including: Chitty Chitty Bang Bang • Good Night • Happy Birthday to You • Heart and Soul • Over the Rainbow • Sing • This Land Is Your Land • and more.
00119636 .... $9.99

Elton John – Greatest Hits
20 of his biggest hits, including: Bennie and the Jets • Candle in the Wind • Crocodile Rock • Rocket Man • Tiny Dancer • Your Song • and more.
00221832 .... $14.99

Les Misérables
14 favorites from the Broadway sensation arranged for beginning pianists. Titles include: At the End of the Day • Bring Him Home • Castle on a Cloud • I Dreamed a Dream • In My Life • On My Own • Who Am I? • and more.
00221812 .... $15.99

The Phantom of the Opera
9 songs from the Broadway spectacular, including: All I Ask of You • Angel of Music • Masquerade • The Music of the Night • The Phantom of the Opera • The Point of No Return • Prima Donna • Think of Me • Wishing You Were Somehow Here Again.
00110006 .... $14.99

Pride & Prejudice
Music from the Motion Picture Soundtrack
12 piano pieces from the 2006 Oscar-nominated film: Another Dance • Darcy's Letter • Georgiana • Leaving Netherfield • Liz on Top of the World • Meryton Townhall • The Secret Life of Daydreams • Stars and Butterflies • and more.
00316125 .... $12.99

The Sound of Music
arranged by Phillip Keveren
9 favorites: Climb Ev'ry Mountain • Do-Re-Mi • Edelweiss • The Lonely Goatherd • Maria • My Favorite Things • Sixteen Going on Seventeen • So Long, Farewell • The Sound of Music.
00316057 .... $10.99

Best of Taylor Swift
A dozen top tunes from this crossover sensation: Fearless • Fifteen • Hey Stephen • Love Story • Our Song • Picture to Burn • Teardrops on My Guitar • White Horse • You Belong with Me • and more.
00307143 .... $12.99

Worship Favorites
20 powerful songs: Above All • Come, Now Is the Time to Worship • I Could Sing of Your Love Forever • More Precious Than Silver • Open the Eyes of My Heart • Shout to the Lord • and more.
00311207 .... $12.99

Complete song lists online at
www.halleonard.com